Supplement ... Brian Skoyles

The introduction you have just read is as written by Kevin, I have made no changes.

Those of you who read the general angling press might be surprised that this new Haynes Manual on Carp Fishing has just been published, because you will be aware that Kevin is no longer with us. Sadly, cruelly, Kevin was taken seriously ill in March 2013 and shortly after his 40th birthday in June he passed away. Kevin was close to finishing this manual when he found out about his illness, and he asked me and Mick Rouse to complete it for him. We were both honoured that Kevin had asked us and vowed to do our best to complete it to the high standards that Kevin always set himself. We hope you think we have achieved that.

Mick and I both worked with Kevin on angling features and fished with him as a friend. He was a loving family man, the ultimate professional angling journalist and although he never made a fuss about it a very talented angler. Kevin worshiped his wife Jo and their two young children Reuben and Theo. Mick and I hope this book becomes one of many treasured memories they have of Kevin.

Thank you for purchasing this manual, and when you catch that carp of your dreams, give Kev a big thumbs up .... He would have loved that!

Brian Skoyles

A lovely family picture of Kev and Jo with Reuben and Theo

Thanks for your help...

Before diving headlong into the world of carp fishing thanks go first to the people who have helped out with the photography for this book – take a bow Mick Rouse, Lloyd Rogers and Steve Broad at Improve Your Coarse Fishing, UK Carp and Angling Times.

Thanks also to the companies who supplied kit for this book and to a number of fisheries who gave me access to their lakes – particular thanks to Dave Mennie, the Miller family, particularly Tony and Jean (millersfrenchcarpandcats.com), Graham Harman at Etang Meunier (etangmeunier.com) and the team at Lemington Lakes in the Cotswolds (lemingtonlakes.co.uk).

Thanks also go to two very special people who have had a formative role in my carp fishing and writing. Brian Skoyles has been a partner on many of my long distance trips and has shared many laughs, while my incredible dad has backed me all the way. His love of fishing has been transplanted into my veins too and his support has been unstinting for 30 years. To say I owe you is the understatement of the year.

But finally this book is for you mum, I know you'd be so proud even if you did think we were all mad!

Kevin

MEET THE CARP

Haynes

Carp Fishing Manual

The step-by-step guide to becoming a better carp angler

Kevin Green

CONTENTS

Introduction

The pursuit of carp is the biggest growth area in fishing, with a growing number of fishermen spending days, nights and even weeks in search of their ultimate prize.

To some anglers, success is only measured in the capture of giant 'space-hopper' sized carp that look more like hippos than fish, while others set their sights far more realistically and are simply happy to be catching lovely hard fighting carp of any size by design.

This manual is aimed squarely at this second group of fishermen, the people who want to learn how to catch carp but aren't obsessed about pounds, ounces, kilos or grams.

The beauty of carp fishing is that it is incredibly varied and your enjoyment of the sport should be measured in much more than the weight of fish you catch. Learning new methods, overcoming tricky challenges, poor weather or new venues that test you in different ways is how your progression as a carp angler should really be measured.

Helping you along the way this book is split into 14 easy-to-read chapters that are bursting with the very latest information that will give you the tips you need to become a better carper.

HERE'S A SNAPSHOT OF WHAT THE HAYNES CARP FISHING MANUAL CONTAINS:

Chapter 1: We look at the carp itself, how it behaves and the different types of fish that we aim to catch.

Chapter 2: Next we look at the specialist tackle that has been engineered to make carp fishing easier and more productive. We cut through the complexity of modern kit so you know what you need and what you don't.

Chapters 3, 4 and 5: Turning our attention to rigs we then look in detail at the business end of your gear, the rig set-up that could ultimately connect you to the fish of your dreams. We show you how to tie perfect rigs that are productive and not simply flashy, our advice will arm you for any situation and once again we explain the terminology that makes many newcomers and learning carpers feel daunted.

Chapters 6 and 7: Bait is the next subject we look at in detail, first by delving into the world of boilies then we study particle baits. This is a subject that baffles many carp anglers, but we cut through the confusion to deliver straight-forward advice that will see carp picking up your baits on a regular basis.

Chapters 8 and 9: Next we consider how you set up your kit when you get to the waterside and then we study how you prepare your swim to make it attractive to carp. This stage is often ignored by many anglers who consider bait and rigs to hold the key to catching fish, but the reality is the most successful anglers are those who can read a situation and adopt the correct approach to what faces them.

Chapter 10: PVA in its various forms is one of the most helpful pieces of modern carp kit and such is its ability to help you catch more fish that it deserves a section all of its own.

Chapter 11: Once you've got a bite the next hurdle is landing and returning the fish successfully and safely. This manual shows you how.

Chapter 12: Catching fish off the surface is one of the most thrilling ways to catch a carp and in this part of the manual we tell you what gear you need, how to make a great rig and the tactics that help you catch.

Chapter 13: If you're an adventurous carper then stalking fish in the margins is going to be right up your street. This commando-style fishing is seat-of-your pants time and when you've learned the basics of carp fishing you've got to give this a go.

Chapter 14: Finally we deliver a snap-shot of quick tips that will move your carp fishing onto a different level. These ideas are easy to follow but very effective.

There you have it then, the outline of a helpful book that is packed with masses of step-by-step tips, that destroy some of the myths that surround carp fishing and which put off so many anglers.

Carp fishing needn't be rocket science, in fact understanding the behaviour of the fish itself is more important to catching them than any rig or bait. When all's said and done a carp is a fish much like any other fish and much of the hocus-pocus that's spouted about the technicality of carp fishing is nothing but hype.

This manual makes carp fishing easy to understand and arms you with the foundation of knowledge that will see you right in 99% of the fishing situations you'll face.

With this stockpile of information at your disposal you'll be in the perfect position to catch fish and enjoy your carp fishing.

My dad Ken. His love of fishing has been transplanted into my veins too and his support has always been unstinting.

Carp are without doubt the most successful species of freshwater fish in the world. From Australia to the Arctic, New York to Normandy and England to Estonia, you can find carp swimming in lakes, rivers and canals in every continent except Antarctica. They've been an incredible success story, and no matter where they've turned up they've proved themselves to be incredibly adaptable, resilient and prolific. This is one of the underlying reasons why they've become so popular in so many countries – anglers everywhere have recognised the fighting prowess and size of this power-packed species.

In this opening chapter we give you a grounding not only in the fish's origins but also in its main behaviour traits. After all, what makes a carp 'tick' plays a crucial part in the overall equation of catching them. Once you understand how your target behaves you know what tactics to use to catch it.

Carp: where did they come from?

Carp have existed for many centuries and there's evidence of them living in various parts of Asia and Europe hundreds of years ago. In the UK carp were 'farmed' as far back as the 14th century, by monks who used them as a valuable food source; the grounds of some ancient monasteries still contain the stew ponds these fish lived in. But during the last century a sea-change has taken place in the very structure of the species thanks to selective breeding, primarily for food purposes.

Compared to the long, lean, fully-scaled fish the monks would've tucked into, the modern carp is something of a Frankenstein creation. Careful breeding by fish farmers has produced carp that have fewer scales, random scale formations and – most importantly – grow much bigger and quicker. Monks didn't eat 20-pounders, let alone the 40lb leviathans that are now caught every week.

What the monks would think of the 101lb World Record fish that broke through the magical 'ton' barrier for the first time in 2012 can only be imagined. They probably wouldn't even recognise it as a carp!

Recognise your carp

One of the main side-effects of the fish-farming industry is that carp have not only got bigger but they've also changed their body shape and the scales that coat their bodies. The pictures here show the eight main types of carp you might catch. Although they look different, all are essentially the same species, although from an angler's perspective we tend to think of grass carp and crucian carp as different species to target.

Common carp

Fully covered with rows of fairly uniform scales, 'the common' most closely resembles the wild carp farmed by the ancient monks. The modern fish, however, grows much faster and much bigger.

A perfect example of a beautiful common carp.

Good friend and top photographer Mick Rouse with a lovely example of a common carp.

Mirror carp

Dotted with randomly sized scales, these fish vary massively in their appearance. The two pictures here show a lightly scaled carp and a more heavily scaled fish, just to demonstrate the variety of patterns you can catch.

Big but lightly scattered scales on an immaculate mirror carp.

A more heavily scaled mirror.

Friend and fellow-carper Brian Skoyles with a lovely linear, with a near-perfect row of scales running down its lateral line.

Linear mirror

This description refers to a specific scale pattern that's found very occasionally on certain mirror carp. In its true sense a 'linear' has an almost uniform row of scales running down the lateral line in the centre of the fish's body. Some anglers call this fish a 'zip linear' due to the pattern of the scales.

Fully-scaled mirror

This version of a mirror carp is patterned, or 'painted', with random-sized scales that are haphazardly scattered across the fish's flanks. A true fully-scaled carp is a rare and especially beautiful fish. At times there can be some confusion between a fully-scaled mirror and a common.

RIGHT: Do they come any prettier than this full-scaled mirror? A true fully scaled mirror carp is a rare and especially beautiful fish.

Ghost carp

This is an ornamental type of carp originally bred for the fish-keeping trade but which has gradually found its way into the angling scene. Usually painted with a metallic black and white colouration, they are striking-looking fish.

LEFT: Lovely example of a ghost carp, which are gradually becoming more widespread.

A true leather has no scales on its body and is a rare fish.

A stunning example of a leather carp from Etang Meunier.

Leather carp

A true 'leather' is an exceptionally rare fish with no scales on its body at all. Many claimed 'leather carp' actually have a few scales on the wrist of their tales or just behind the gill plate. A genuine leather is coated in skin and nothing else.

Koi carp

Another relatively modern 'creation' of the fish-keeping trade, these vividly-coloured ornamental fish have also crept into the angling scene. There are huge variations in koi colouration, from bright orange through to black and red.

RIGHT: A stunning koi and a 'Harry Potter' impersonation.

Grass carp

A relatively rare carp that behaves very differently to the other main carp species. A fish that often picks through weed (hence it's name) and has a beaky mouth to help it pick up individual food items. In recent years they've shown more adaptability than many gave them credit for, and in some waters they get caught with standard carping tactics.

LEFT: Martyn Skoyles with a superb example of a grass carp. More and more of these are being caught by standard carping tactics.

How do carp behave?

One of the key reasons why carp have proved so prolific and successful is their ability to adapt to different conditions. Although they feed mainly in the warmer months they will feed throughout the year, and can go into a state of virtual suspended animation to conserve energy stocks in the worst weather. Carp often live for 20 to 30 years, but individual fish are known to have kept swimming for over 50 years – very few freshwater species get close to this longevity.

As for how they feed and what they'll eat, well, that varies hugely. Their telescopic mouth is primarily designed for hoovering up food items off the lake bed – bloodworm, water snails, shrimps and our baits are their staple foods. Unlike fish such as chub and roach that pick up individual food items with their lips, carp literally hoover up their food, sucking in mouthfuls of silt and debris along with edible food items. A special filtering process allows them to spit out the rubbish and digest their meal. This explains why the standard way to catch carp is with some type of leger rig that presents a bait hard on the bottom, where the fish do so much of their feeding – in this manual you'll find a host of rigs that place your bait in the carp's main dining room.

But these fish will also look up for their food – they can suck flies and other food items off the surface, and pick off suspended items of food that are floating in mid-water. The fact that carp feed at any part of the water column also explains why certain rigs, baits and tactics have been devised

Their telescopic mouths are primarily designed for hoovering up food off the bottom.

to fish on the surface and at any depth between the top and the bottom.

Above all, the fact that carp suck up their food rather than physically picking it up in their lips is a subtle difference that explains why some sort of hair rig has become 'the way' to catch fish. As you'll see later in the manual, attaching your bait to a piece of line hanging below the hook (the hair), rather than actually placing it on the hook, has become the dominant way to catch carp in the modern era. While many anglers do slip their bait directly on to the hook, those trying to catch specimen carp very rarely do so – modern rigs are purpose-made to take advantage of how big carp feed.

Carp are also skilled at taking food mid-water and off the top.

RIGHT: Despite what the old books say, we now know that carp can still be caught in the winter.

Feeding times

There was a time when carp fishing in winter was the preserve of a lunatic fringe. Many people believed they were uncatchable in the cold, and it was widely speculated that they actually hibernated. We now know that this is rubbish. Carp feed throughout the year, and although you may have to adapt your tactics a little it's possible to catch them in just about all weather.

As a general guide, April to November is the main catching period. Warmer water temperatures stimulate natural food, which in turn encourages the carp to keep moving and burn energy that needs replacing. However, it's still possible to catch fish in the winter months utilising a more focused approach that offers the fish a smaller amount of food in precise locations. Many of the high-attract baits we'll deal with later in the book come into their own in winter, as they're a strong stimulus to fish that might be reluctant to move and feed.

There's also a belief among a considerable number of anglers that carp are nocturnal feeders – they quote the fact that so many fish are caught at night as evidence that fish don't feed during the day at many venues. There's even a saying that certain lakes are 'night waters', meaning they're a waste of time during daylight. But don't make the mistake

of accepting this on your lake. The truth is that carp can and do feed at all times of the day or night. It's almost certain that lots of them get caught at night simply because they can't see the rig or the angler, or because bank-side disturbance is greatly reduced and they feel more confident.

It might be the case that you have to work a bit harder for your fish during daylight hours and try a different tactic, but never make the mistake of presuming you can only catch big fish by bivvying up for nights on end and chalking up mammoth hours on the bank. I've fished many so-called 'night waters' where I've repeatedly stalked carp in the margins on bright and hot summer days.

However, it is true that light levels and weather conditions do influence carp's feeding behaviour. As a general rule they feed best during overcast, windy and mild conditions, with the early hours of the morning often being a particularly good window for action. Warm and sunny conditions will tend to draw the fish higher in the water column, and surface feeding is usually restricted to the warmest months.

But for every 'rule' like this you'll find a counter trend – for example, on many lakes in the middle of winter you'll often find carp shoaled up in mid-water, and a bait presented there is often a good bet.

This is one of the aspects of carp fishing that's most attractive – the target fish can be very unpredictable, and an unusual approach can often pay off spectacularly.

LEFT: The early hours of the morning are often a particularly productive time, so it can pay to get up early.

Meet the eating machine

One of the things that most characterises carp is their great ability to hunt out food – they have great senses of smell, taste and sight, and you'll need to bear this in mind when you consider how your bait works and why making your rigs stealthy will get you more bites. And don't forget carp often have a fear of things that go 'bump', and loud noises that advertise your presence.

Smell

Carp have two flaps of skin standing upright on the front of their snout. These cover two small holes that pass into the

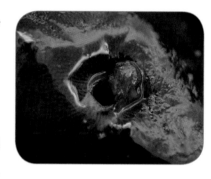

fish's head. Water passes down these two channels and comes into contact with something called the olfactory rosette. This complex, folded structure is packed with cells that are incredibly sensitive to the chemical and aromatic signals given off by natural food items and, of course, anglers' baits.

The chemical signals that carp are especially sensitive to are called amino acids, given off by natural food items and extracts that are incorporated in carp baits. These messages scream 'food' to a carp. This explains why baits that have a subtle 'natural' smell might outperform bait loaded with artificial flavour. Research has shown that carp can detect some aminos at levels of one part per trillion – that's the equivalent of one teaspoon-full of chemical diluted in 2,000 swimming pools!

Be in no doubt – carp have got a great sense of smell.

Taste

Humans taste food through the buds on their tongue. Carp, on the other hand, have taste buds in their mouth, on their lips, their barbules, gill rakers, head and even their fins!

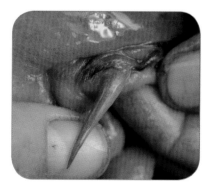

Inside the mouth carp also have something called the palatal organ. This is a fleshy pad that's packed with taste sensors and actually helps with the sorting of food. As a carp sucks up the

surface of the lake bed the food and debris are hoovered up at the same time, and it's the job of the palatal organ to help with sorting this material so that the edible items are digested and the rubbish is spat back out again.

The carp's sense of taste is less sensitive than its ability to smell, and the taste buds are only activated when they actually touch something edible.

It's also a fact that the pH level of the fishery will have an effect on what the carp tastes. This explains why one bait is unlikely to conquer all waters at all times of the year – which is why having a few options when you go fishing is always a good idea.

Sight

Debate still rages regarding what carp can actually see. However, it's generally agreed that carp have got a good sense of vision, and although lots of colours will appear as shades they can clearly define contrasting colours very well. This is why bright-coloured baits, or baits that stand out from the others in the swim – so-called 'target baits' – can trigger a carp's curiosity.

It's also clear that carp can spot crude end tackle, and the more fish are fished for, the more they avoid cumbersome rigs or lines that are cutting through the water. Carp are also able to pick out movement, which explains why keeping off the skyline and not moving around much can be crucial when trying to catch carp in the margins. For example, fish swimming near the surface will often spook when a shadow darts across the water – their sense of self-preservation is strong.

So while many anglers dress in camouflage to avoid spooking fish, this is pointless if they move around a lot – it would probably be better to stalk in a pink shirt and stand still than to dress like a tree and move around a lot!

Sound

Like many coarse fish, carp have a great sense of hearing thanks to the lateral line that runs down their flank and picks up vibrations, plus a hidden ear structure inside their head that's also very sensitive to noise. This explains why stealthy anglers often catch more fish than those who make excessive noise.

In modern carp fishing a great deal of importance is placed on the science of bait composition and rig engineering, but the fact is that simply being quiet and not alerting the carp to your presence can often be a critical and very underrated skill.

THE SPECIALIST TACKLE

Picking the right rod

One of the most obvious choices you must make when you go carp fishing is the rod you do it with. Carp rods are specialist pieces of kit that have been purpose-made for landing big fish and for casting large legers or bait spods.

Here are the key factors you should look at when choosing a rod:

Length

Carp rods are available at different lengths, but in most cases a 12ft rod is ideal. This is a good length for solid casting performance and fish playing. You'll find that many rod ranges are almost exclusively available as 12ft models, and in the vast majority of cases that is the perfect length for most anglers to pick. However, if you mainly fish at short range, the venue you visit is heavily vegetated with narrow swims or you're not a particularly big-framed person, a shorter rod of 10ft or 11ft may be more comfortable for you.

Likewise, if you're a man mountain or you're fishing an inland sea where long-range casting is going to be essential, then a 13-footer may be a better option for you.

Incidentally, when you fish always make sure that the two sections of your rod are lined up so that the line flies through the guides smoothly. This maximises your casting performance.

Fittings

Make sure your rod has a quality screw-down reel seat that secures the reel firmly and won't come undone while you're battling a fish. You also want a rod that's fitted with strong guides that have top-quality ceramic linings, so that the line slips through them with minimum friction. This means that casting and fish-playing performance is maximised.

As for the butt of the rod, some feature cork handles while others have abbreviated foam grips or rubberised coatings. Frankly it doesn't matter which you pick; this is purely down to personal taste and – dare I say it – fashion. As any newcomer will soon realise, picking carp fishing tackle can easily be influenced by what's deemed fashionable at the time, but try not to get sucked in by this. Pick the gear that works for you and, most importantly, does the job you need it to do. Don't get obsessed with having the latest kit that looks the business – chasing carp-fishing fashion will needlessly cost you a fortune, and will distract you from the skills that actually put fish on the bank.

Test curve/action

This is the big factor that should influence the rod you pick – in simple terms, how powerful is it and how does it bend?

All carp rods have a test curve attached to them, which is a measurement of the weight that needs to be attached to the rod tip to make it bend through 90° plus. Typically most carp rods are rated in the 2lb to 3.5lb test curve (TC) range – the higher the test curve the stiffer and more powerful the rod. In recent years carp rods have tended to become more powerful with higher test-curve ratings: this is in recognition of the fact

Does it have the potential to cast your chosen rig/bait to where you hope to fish?

that many anglers cast 80–100 yards plus, and that they're casting out heavier set-ups adorned with PVA bags (see pages 132–139).

As a general guide a test curve of 2.75lb to 3lb will suit most normal fishing situations at most venues. However, if you're fishing smaller fisheries where the fishing is done at close range a 2lb or 2.5lb TC rod may be more than capable of casting the required distance and will be more enjoyable to play hooked fish on, as it'll be softer and more forgiving than a beefier rod. Likewise, if all your fishing is going to be at long range, with casting well in excess of 100 or 120 yards then a 3.25lb or 3.5lb rod may be a better pick.

When choosing just try to be sensible about the type of fishing you're most likely to do, and what type of caster you are. If you're still learning the ropes, picking a super-stiff, very powerful rod would be a poor choice – you simply won't have the casting skill to 'wind-up' the potential power of such an out-and-out casting rod.

A 12ft rod with a test curve of 2.75lb to 3lb is perfect for the vast majority of carp anglers.

Quality

The amount of money you spend on your rod can vary hugely, but as with many items of fishing tackle the general rule is not to buy the cheapest gear unless you have to, and not to get too worried about the top-end tackle until you're really proficient. Mid-price range rods from reputable companies like Daiwa, Fox, Nash, Shimano, JRC and E-S-P won't let you down.

Specialist rods

While the general advice given above is right for the vast majority of carp fishing situations, there are some exceptions. For a start many companies produce specialist spod/marker float rods that are specially strengthened to cope with the demands of casting fully loaded spods or marker floats (see chapters 8 and 9).

While not essential as you start carp fishing, they'll soon become a standard part of your kit, and buying such a rod from any of the reputable companies noted above will serve you well.

If you go on to get involved in stalking carp in the margins you'll also find picking a very short 7–10ft rod of 2.5–2.75lb is a huge help. Chapter 13 deals with this type of tool in greater detail, but if you see 'stalking' rods in the tackle shop, this is what they're used for.

Be sensible with your rod choice. A 12ft rod with a test curve of 2.75lb to 3lb is perfect for the vast majority of carp angling situations.

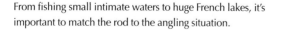

From fishing small intimate waters to huge French lakes, it's important to match the rod to the angling situation.

Picking the right reel

There's a wide range of reels suitable for carp fishing, from the middle-size 4,000s to 'big pits'.

There are many different types of fixed spool reels that can be used for carp fishing. Here we look at what the choices are, how you make your selection and how you fill it with line so that you get the very best performance from it.

Freespool reels

This type of reel features a special drag system, which can be preset to allow line to be released from the spool under a certain pressure when a carp picks up and runs with your bait – this is why Shimano, who invented the system, called it 'Baitrunner'. Not only does this stop your rod getting dragged into the water by a charging carp but it also places a degree of control on the fish from the moment it's hooked and bolts. The resistance offered by the freespool system slows the fish down and saps some of its energy straight

from the off. The other advantage of this system is that it's engaged and disengaged with the flick of a lever on the back of the reel or disengaged by turning the reel handle.

A 4,000 to 6,000 size freespool reel will suffice for the vast majority of anglers. Once you've learned how to fill the reel and cast properly, reels of this size will be capable of hitting the 100-yard range. Freespool reels also balance with most carp rods, as they aren't too heavy and tend to have smaller handles that are comfortable to use and wind.

Things to look out for are how tight the freespool system can be locked down – in some circumstances, such as when you're fishing in thick weed or you're casting near to snags, you'll want to fish 'locked up' with a tightly set freespool system. Some reels can't be locked up tightly enough, but most reels from leading manufacturers are well designed.

This type of reel features a special drag system that can be preset to allow line to be released from the spool under a certain pressure when a carp picks up and runs with your bait – this is why Shimano, who invented the system, called it 'Baitrunner'.

Secondly, check out the quality of the bearings and gearing, as they take a lot of hammering, and finally look at the drag system. When you're playing a carp (see Chapter 11) it's far smoother to release line on the drag than it is to backwind the reel handle to let it out manually. My personal preference is to go for a front-drag reel – I find them smoother and easier to adjust – but you may prefer rear-drag models.

As with the rod you buy, it makes sense not to skimp on what you pay. For the last 20 years I've used Daiwa and Shimano freespool reels and have been impressed with all of them.

Big pit reels

As carp fishing has developed in recent years more specialist kit has become available to aid longer-range casting – this is where the trend to use bigger reels has come from. Often called 'big pit' reels due to the fact they were made to be used on vast lakes where long-range casting is the norm, more anglers now use these reels whatever range they're fishing at.

If you're likely to go long-range casting, or you can only afford one set of reels to do all your fishing with, buying a set of big pits might well be the best idea. Just be aware that these big reels tend to be heavier and aren't quite as nice to use as a smaller reel.

You can buy big pits that have a freespool system on them, such as the Daiwa Infinity that I've used for many years and rate very highly. However, in recent years several high-

LEFT: The Daiwa Infinity Big Pit has a free spool facility. It's a reel I've used for many years and rate very highly.

BELOW: Big pits with a free spool facility have become much more affordable.

performance 'big pits' have been launched that have moved carp reel design a big step forward. Taking technology designed for tournament casting, where gaining an inch on the cast might make the difference between winning and coming second, these reels are made from high-tech materials that produce lightweight reels and superb line-lay on the spool.

The tension can be adjusted from locked to slack in less than a single turn of the mechanism.

The very best of these reels have become a hybrid – although they don't have a full-blown freespool system fitted they do have a quick-drag system that allows the tension to be adjusted from locked to slack in less than one full turn of the mechanism. As they're at the forefront of fishing technology these reels are inevitably expensive, but products like the Daiwa Basia QDX are the sports cars of carp fishing and almost as glamorous!

Due to their casting performance big pit reels are also used for spodding and marker float work, as you'll see in Chapter 9.

At the forefront of technology, the Daiwa Basia QDX, the sports car of carp fishing reels.

How to fill your reel with line

Casting performance and fish-playing ability alike are hindered by a poorly loaded reel, so it's vital to get it right. This series of pictures shows you different ways to fill your reel with line properly.

First, ask yourself: 'Do I need the spool backing up?' – by which I mean, you need to make a decision on how much line you need on the spool. Most reels have a capacity far in excess of what you actually need, so it might be possible to reduce the capacity with some backing. 'Backing' is where you wind on some old line and tape over it, so that you use less actual reel line each time you spool up. It can be a much better plan both economically and tactically to back up spools, as you can then change line more often without it costing so much.

Knot your main line on to the spool

It's always good practice to securely knot your mainline to the spool. I recommend using a grinner knot tied around the mainline to form a strong slip knot. Make sure as you pull the slip knot tight that you position it at the base of the spool. (For grinner knot see page184).

Use a slip knot made with a grinner knot around the mainline.

As you pull the slip knot tight make sure it ends up at the bottom of the spool.

Winding on the line method 1 (from warm water)

This is a very popular method, as the warm water makes the line very easy to manage. Simply take a bucket, fill with warm water and drop the spool into it. After a few minutes wind it on to the spool … easy!

Winding on the line method 2 (with the help of a third party)

Another popular method is to get a bit of help by getting a third party to control the spool for you. Just get them to thread the spool on to a screwdriver or something similar, then as you wind they can control the pressure on the spool for you.

Winding on the line method 3 (with a winding attachment)

If you have a small space spare on a shed or garage wall this little gadget will be helpful. Just slide the spool on, adjust the spring tension and wind on.

Remember, whatever system you choose, make sure the spools are fully loaded. It will make a massive difference to your casting efficiency and make playing fish easier.

Gearing up for night fishing

One of the things that sets carp fishermen apart from most other anglers is that we stay out at night and keep on fishing.

However, in order to fish through the night, regardless of how cold or wet it is, you need to have the right kit, and a bivvy tent is essential. While there are dozens of bivvies on the market, these pages will show you three basic designs and look at the pros and cons of each.

'Pram-hood'-style bivvy

This form of fishing tent is constructed around a central frame that's erected or collapsed by being folded like the hood on a pram. The main advantages of this system are that it's quick to set up and produces a very rigid set-up with

a strong metal frame running through the fabric of the tent. No wonder pram-hood-style bivvies are so popular.

If there's a downside to this type of bivvy, it's that it tends to be heavier than some others due to the metal frame. Many of them are also quite big and can be difficult to squeeze into tight swims. Nevertheless, pram hood bivvies are easy to use and practical.

Pop-up bivvy

A variety of bivvies are available that feature some kind of mechanism that springs up or folds out and locks into place. The best of these are excellent choices, as they're easy to set up – they come out of the bag and are simply folded out to form the tent. Many of these designs also feature a twin-skin

design, where there's an inner tent and an outer shell that's warmer at night and reduces condensation. Again, these tents tend to be quite bulky and can be heavy, but the more expensive pop-up bivvies are extremely practical.

Brolly systems

The final style of bivvy is based around using an oversized umbrella. These systems are designed to be quick to set up, relatively lightweight, and ideally suited to a mobile or short-session style of fishing. Some, like the Nash Titan (pictured), look like a brolly but actually have an inbuilt frame that simply folds open when it comes out of the bag.

Brolly systems are easy to set up and ideal if you're likely to move swims regularly, but they don't offer the comfort and protection against the elements that a bigger bivvy offers.

Bedchair and sleeping bag

As well as a bivvy, don't forget you'll need a bedchair and sleeping bag. If you're planning to go night fishing, it's vital to have an adjustable and comfortable sprung bedchair and a sleeping bag that keeps you warm.

It's important you don't cut corners with what you pick. Spend enough money to get you a bed that's comfortable to sleep on and a four-season sleeping bag to use with it. It's surprising how cold it can get at night, even in the warmer months, and if you're cold or uncomfortable, you won't fish efficiently.

The other kit you need

That's the major items of kit described. Now we'll provide a guide to the other key equipment you'll need and what you should look for.

Bite alarms

Dozens of electronic bite alarms are available and most are very good. The rod and reel is placed on these indicators after you've cast out, to signal the movement of the line when a carp picks up the bait. Depending on what your budget is you'll be able to pick alarms that have adjustable

Bite alarms are essential on longer sessions so that you get quickly on to your rods when they signal a take. Most of my friends use either the Fox or Delkim systems.

volume, tone or sensitivity. The best models allow you to adjust all three and even have a remote control sounder box that can be placed inside the bivvy to help you respond to a bite at night.

Indicators

There's a huge range of indicators that you can clip on your line to help you understand what's happening in the water. I'm a fan of 'hangers', so-called because they do just that. They hang on the line and help show line movement, moving up as a fish moves away from you and dropping down if a fish moves towards you ('drop-backs'). They can

Indicators attached to the line can help show fish movement when it picks up a bait, and fish activity in the swim.

also be useful for showing fish activity in your swim. Slight movements up and straight down are what are known as line bites, caused when fish catch your line as they swim past it. It can be a great way of knowing if fish are present in your baited area – the downside being that fish bumping into your line can be spooked and leave the area.

How much of a drop you need to the hanger is usually dictated by how you want to use them. Some carpers like to fish the line relatively tight with the hangers up near the rod, considered better for drop-backs and for fishing at range; others have them much lower, with the line slack, which is better when fishing close in, as the slacker line doesn't scare the fish.

Rod pod/bank sticks

Bite alarms are screwed into bank sticks and pushed into the ground to provide a solid frame for your rods to sit on after casting. Go for a quality bank stick, as over a season they have to cope with a lot of different bank-side conditions, from baked mud to gravel. I really like the ones that have a screw-in system at the end, as they can help the stick get purchase in the ground.

On some lakes the swims you fish from have either very hard banks, gravelled areas or wooden platforms that bank sticks can't be pushed into. This is where a stand-alone rod pod proves to be extremely useful.

Landing net

Carp can be big, and a landing net with a minimum of 42in arms is essential to give you enough mesh to scoop up the fish you hook. Beware of sub-standard nets that have flexible and flimsy arms and pole – to help you net a fish and avoid breakages you need a rigid set-up, so avoid the cheaper options. They'll almost certainly cost you more in the long run, as this book will ensure you're catching plenty of fish that will find out a poor quality net!

Unhooking mat

It's a sensible rule on most responsible fisheries that you must use an unhooking mat when carp fishing. Some mats are basically soft, thickly padded cushions filled with foam or poly balls. These cushion the fish from damage when it's on the bank, and as long as you buy from a reputable company like Nash, Fox, Daiwa, Chub or JRC then you'll get a good product.

Other mats are a bit more complicated and are generally referred to as 'cradles'. These mats have a solid frame from which a cushioned mat is hung, in which the fish lays as if in a hammock, which keeps it suspended off the floor and protected from damage. In Chapter 11 you'll see this product in action.

Carp cradles are becoming very popular and are a real aid to fish care.

Chair

A low chair is a really useful accessory to your carp fishing tackle, as long as you use it properly – this means you sit on it facing the water and you study the surface for signs of fish while you're fishing.

Clothing

The days of putting on an extra pair of jeans in winter and an anorak if it rains are gone. Firms like Nash, Fox, Sundridge, Diem and E-S-P produce purpose-made clothing that should keep you warm and dry and maintain your fishing performance.

You won't fish well if you're cold and wet, whereas you will if you feel comfortable. That way you can be out there fishing in a wild south-westerly that's whipping the water to a froth and making the carp feed like

With top-quality warm and waterproof clothing you fish better, and cope better with whatever the weather throws at you.

mad. It might seem over the top to say that good-quality clothing can help you catch more fish, but if you're out there when other anglers are tucked up at home listening to the wind roaring, you'll be the one holding the fish!

This 47lb winter fish was a lake record for the Acton Burnell Top Lake when I caught it. It was caught in lashing rain and gale force winds, and if I hadn't had the right clothing I probably wouldn't even have been at the water!

On a long session you fish better if you feel warm and well fed. A small stove is a real aid to achieving this, especially in the colder months. Having a brew on the bank is a tradition well worth maintaining!

Cooking gear

For much the same reason as you need the right clothing, it's also vital to have a stove to prepare cooked meals and hot drinks and to keep yourself energised. As a young carper I used to live on the most meagre rations, but it did me no good. Carrying a lightweight Primus gas stove and bottle is a true essential.

Head torch

There's nothing worse than using a torch excessively when night fishing – other anglers hate it, and it's possible that fish will actually get spooked by flashes of light darting across the surface. However, a three to five LED head torch is vital to help with baiting of rigs and unhooking fish. Having a head torch rather than an ordinary

torch leaves your hands free to do the vital job of extracting the hook from a fish.

Trolley

This is another piece of tackle that not so long ago was seen as a luxury but has become more and more regarded as an essential. Walk on to any carp water and you'll see an awful lot of anglers with trolleys parked near their bivvies.

There are two reasons for using a trolley to transport your gear to a swim. Most obviously they simply take the strain of carting a mountain of heavy tackle, meaning you can get to the water quickly, get to distant swims you might struggle to

reach and not suffer a coronary getting there! The picture shows a Nash Trax Barrow, and as you can see its luggage has been designed to fit the frame, to make transportation of kit quick and easy.

There's another less obvious reason for using a trolley, and it's one that many of the very best anglers embody – *mobility*. The ability to load your kit on a trolley and switch swims quickly means you can move around a lake far quicker than doing it on foot with all your gear on your back. If you're keeping an eye on the surface and constantly looking for signs of carp activity, this can be vital. If you spot fish topping in an area and act on these signs by moving swims quickly, you'll often catch fish that you simply wouldn't have caught if you'd stayed put.

So while a trolley may seem simply a means to get your tackle to the water, if it's used properly, it can actually help to catch more fish.

Moving on

In the opening two chapters of this manual we've dealt with many of the core basics – the foundation stones that set you up for becoming a good carp angler. If you understand the fish you're targeting and kit yourself out with the right tackle you've taken a good step towards being a carp angler.

Now it's time to delve into the complicated world of carp rigs – the hook, line and legers that you use at the business end to catch a carp. Over the next few chapters I'll detail the top rigs that'll suit the vast majority of fishing situations. There are many other rigs that can be tried, but they're

essentially advanced set-ups that are primarily suitable for very specialist situations.

Just remember, though – rigs *aren't* the answer to catching carp. Many newcomers (and plenty of experienced anglers too) mistakenly place excessive faith in the ability of a rig to catch them a carp. It won't. A rig will only work for you when it's cast into the right location, at the right time, with a bait the carp want to eat. Never forget that. Your ability to read the behaviour of the carp and put your rig in front of feeding fish is far more important than the rig itself.

CARP RIGS: THE BASICS

Carp rigs have become a science, and some set-ups look more like Christmas trees than lean and efficient fish catchers. High-tech lines and braids, unusually-shaped hooks and legers and a host of intricate pieces of moulded plastic and metalware characterise many modern carp rigs. Walk into many tackle shops now and you'll see walls filled with boards of carp rig components. It's no wonder many anglers find themselves baffled by the latest rigs.

In this chapter you'll get a grounding in the main items of rig-making kit to set you up for tying your own rigs that will catch loads of fish.

Picking the right mainline

The line you load on your reel is important, and there are three materials to choose from: nylon, fluorocarbon and braid. Let's look at the advantages and disadvantages of each.

Nylon

First you've got standard nylon monofilamen. There are literally dozens of brands on the market and many modern lines are exceptionally good.

For most carp fishing situations lines like these (see picture below) are perfect. For smaller carp in fisheries free of snags you can opt for a minimum of 10lb breaking strain with 12lb and 15lb versions a more sensible option for medium to longer range casting, say up to 100yds, and waters that contain plenty of weeds, lilies, reeds or overhanging trees.

Many carp waters have a 'minimum breaking strain' of line that anglers must use and you'll usually find 12lb is the basic requirement. In most cases I use 15lb mono for the extra security it gives.

In exceptional circumstances lighter mainlines can be used, for example, if you are surface fishing with softer rods

and lighter hooklink lines for example, then the mainline can be stepped down to 10lb.

Likewise if you are looking to fish at extreme range, well past the 100yd mark, you often need to reduce the strength and diameter of your mainline to maximise the range you can reach. A mainline of 8lb has a much lower diameter than 15lb line, not only does this reduce the drag of the line as it

There are lots of nylon lines to select from. Just make sure you pick a reliable brand from a well-known manufacturer, and ask about the properties.

Whatever brand you pick you'll probably need two or three different breaking strains.

flies through the rod rings but it also has massively reduced resistance in the air as your leger rig blasts across the lake.

A rig will fly much further when it is cast on lighter, thinner line although to cope with this you will need to use something called a shock leader. In chapter 8 we'll deal with this in detail but this is basically a link of heavy-duty line that is sandwiched between the mainline and the leger to take the strain of the cast and absorb the power that would snap the light line loaded on the reel. This is very much specialist carp fishing as a great deal of practice is needed to cast extreme ranges safely and a great deal of care taken in playing fish on the lighter line.

In the vast majority of situations a nylon mono of 12lb or 15lb is a perfect choice. When teamed with a 2oz to 3oz leger the line is strong enough to withstand all but the most violent casts and it has enough abrasion resistance to cope with underwater vegetation and snags.

Fluorocarbon

The second choice of mainline is a product called fluorocarbon, which is becoming increasingly popular. Although it looks very much like traditional nylon this line is thicker, stiffer and much heavier for its respective breaking strain.

While it doesn't cast as smoothly as most nylon lines there are two reasons for picking fluorocarbon. Thanks to its high-tech construction, when fluorocarbon is in water it has the same refractive index as daylight, which means it virtually

vanishes. This is an ideal form of camouflage, and fluorocarbon is consequently widely used in clear-water pits where streetwise fish are line-shy and will spook at the very sight of line cutting through the water.

The second reason for using fluorocarbon is the fact that it sinks like a brick. Many anglers using fluorocarbon let their line fall slack after casting so that it'll drop to the bottom and run along the contours of the lake bed. Again, this results in a stealthy presentation, and carp find it difficult to spot anything suspicious, which makes it perfect for clear water lakes and venues where the fish are wised up to spotting or feeling lines and are spooked by anything remotely unusual.

Fluorocarbons have got more user-friendly in recent years, and although they don't cast as far as an identical breaking strain of nylon line, keeping the spool wet aids casting performance and reduces the chance of this wiry line tangling on the cast.

Braid

The final choice of reel line is braid (sometimes called a 'superline'). Braid lines are an expensive and advanced product made with high-tech filaments that have been woven or fused together to form an exceptionally thin and strong line. But it's one that's best used in specialist circumstances.

Because braid doesn't stretch and has a much thinner diameter than any other type of line it can be used for extreme-range fishing – more casting power is transmitted to the leger, and the lower resistance of the braid flying through the air means the rig travels further. Its lack of stretch also means braid is a good choice when using a marker float to gauge the depth or map out the bottom of the lake (see Chapter 8). It's also good when spodding out bait (explained in Chapter 9), as the strength of such a low-diameter line is unbeatable for punching out a loaded bait rocket.

However, braid isn't welcomed on many lakes, as its lack of stretch and sharp edge when under tension has been blamed for causing damage to hooked fish. Many anglers who do try braid on their fishing rods soon back away from it, as the total lack of stretch means it's very easy to bounce fish off the hook.

As a rule, only use braid on your marker float and spod rods, not the fishing rods themselves.

LEFT: Fluorocarbon is thicker and stiffer than nylon, and is popular because it sinks quickly.

BELOW: Braids are very much a specialist option. They're thinner than nylon, with no stretch.

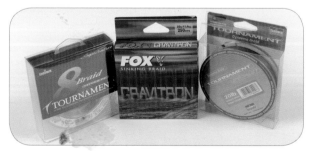

Understanding legers

Leads come in all shapes and sizes.

The pear/square pear casts reasonably well, and doesn't roll over the lake bed.

There are dozens of different shapes, sizes and finishes of leger. The following is a guide to the main types and explains when and why you use them. All the leads here are available in different sizes, but as a general guide a 2oz to 3oz size is ideal for most situations, with a 3oz lead used on a 3lb test-curve rod and a 2.5oz lead best used on 2.5lb to 2.75lb test-curve rods.

Distance

Aerodynamically shaped for greater casting performance, these legers are best used when your priority is to cast a long way. The downside of a leger like this is that the weight is evenly distributed over its length. This reduces the resistance a fish feels when it picks up your hookbait, and may diminish the likelihood of the fish pricking itself on the hook point. Casting distance leads into shallow water, where the lake bed is very soft and silty, may also mean the rig rockets deep into the bottom, and the hookbait becomes buried.

The distance lead is aerodynamic, to help cast it a long way.

Pear/square pear

This dumpy design increases the resistance to a fish picking up your bait and makes it more likely the fish will hook itself and give you a screaming take, with line pouring off the reel. Although they don't cast as efficiently as distance legers they're still reasonably aerodynamic, fly well through the air and can be cast a long way. Some legers are flattened to prevent them rolling on steep underwater gravel bars or margin slopes.

Inline

Unlike the first two designs of leger, which are attached to the rig via a swivel located at one end, the inline lead was traditionally threaded on to the mainline with the line running through the centre of it. However, as you'll see in Chapter 5, modern inline legers are made where the lead can detach from the line if it becomes snagged in weed. This

Inline leads are usually threaded on to the mainline, and are ideal for use with PVA bags.

greatly increases the chance of you landing a hooked fish. This shape of leger is especially useful when making solid PVA bags, as you'll see in Chapter 10.

Camouflaged leads

It can be a good idea to leave your leads in a flavour soak so that they help attract fish to your hookbait.

lump of soil, and Solar's Weed Effect leads look like a lump of weed. Some anglers also leave their leads in a flavour/ attractor soak, which not only provides casting distance but also helps attract fish to the area around the hookbait. This is especially useful in winter.

'Camo' leads come in a range of shapes and disguises to hide the lead on whatever set of bottom conditions you're fishing on.

Most modern legers are coated in plastic or painted to reduce their profile and make them less obvious to wary fish. However, some designs take this to an extreme level and may give you a slight edge on clear water lakes or if you're fishing for tackle-shy fish. Clear legers are said to disappear. Atomic's heavily coated Dung Bombs look like a random

Specialist leads

Flat, hollow leads with dimples on the edge are used in rivers or on steep gravel bars or sloping margins where you don't want the rig to roll into a tangled heap once it's cast in. Legers with points jutting out from them are used for feature finding and reading the texture of the lake bed – as they're bumped across the bottom the points register what it's made out of.

Types of hooklink material

Just like mainlines, hooklinks come in a wide range of materials.

The material from which you make the final few inches of your rig has a major bearing on how many carp you catch. The way that last bit of line moves and its properties – especially its strength, suppleness, stiffness and abrasion resistance – have a fundamental influence on whether a carp picks up your bait and what you catch. Of all the decisions you make, what type of hooklink you use is one of the most important.

So before we get into the chapters that show you how to tie rigs, here's an explanation of what these different materials are, when you use them and why.

Braid

Soft, strong, camouflaged and very thin braid is the supplest of all hooklink materials, and that's why it's become so

popular in recent years. The woven high-tech filaments that construct a modern braid are so soft and flexible that they give the hookbait an almost identical degree of movement to the free offerings you feed to attract carp to your rig.

With braided hooklinks often coloured to match the lake beds found in different venues, these lines are often said to catch the wariest of fish. If fish can't spot the 'odd-one-out' that has a hook attached to it, then they're far less likely to reject the bait.

While the flexibility and camouflaging of braid are huge advantages the suppleness of the line can be a disadvantage too, as it increases the likelihood of casting tangles since the line can easily wrap around the mainline or leger in flight. To guarantee the rig enters the water untangled and gives the hookbait perfect presentation it's necessary to use anti-tangle measures such as tubing, leaders or PVA bags. We'll look at these measures later.

Some braids can also loop up off the bottom, a presentation that looks very obvious and can spook wary fish. Again this must be countered, or sinking braids must be picked. Use a material like this and the braid can lie smoothly over any undulations on the bottom, adding to the stealth qualities of your rig.

Coated braid

This is a line designed to tackle the main problem of using soft braid, namely, the fact that it can easily tangle. It's a two-piece line that features a soft braided core material with a thin plastic outer coating to stiffen it and make it less likely to tangle on the cast.

One of the great things about coated braids is that the plastic sheath can easily be stripped away to expose the braid and therefore utilise the suppleness at the core of the line. As you'll see, a common use of coated braids is to peel off the

last few inches of line near the hook while leaving the rest of the hooklink stiffened with plastic. This gives the angler the best of both worlds, a partially stiff line that doesn't tangle and a partially soft line that allows the hookbait to behave naturally. Consequently coated braids have probably become the most popular of all hooklink materials.

Nylon

In many ways nylon mono-filament is the direct opposite of braided lines. It's much thicker for the same breaking strain and stiffer too, a fact that makes the hookbait on the end behave far less like the free offerings

you feed with. Many carp anglers therefore consider nylon line to be outdated as a hooklink material.

However, while it appears to be an obvious decision to dismiss nylon line in favour of a softer material, the choice becomes less clear-cut when you consider that many modern nylons are extremely difficult to see in water and can therefore trick wary carp. Nylon lines are also far less tangle-prone due to their relative stiffness, a fact that encourages their use for long-range casting where you want to minimise the drag on your rig in order to maximise the distance it casts. If you don't need to add tubing or a PVA bag to your rig to stop it tangling you'll cast further. The stiffness of nylon can also make it far harder for carp to eject the hookbait when they pick it up. This is why the so-called 'stiff rig' can be productive.

Finally, the development of nylon in recent years has meant lines are now available that are much thinner and softer than they were a few years ago. Although they aren't as flexible as braid, they certainly aren't tow-rope stiff either. Combine this with their camouflage properties and you can see that nylon lines are far from finished as hooklinks.

Fluorocarbon

In Chapter 2 we discussed the benefits of loading fluorocarbon line on your reel. Many of the same properties influencing that choice also count towards using these materials as a hooklink.

The main reason for using fluorocarbon line is that it virtually disappears in water and is therefore almost impossible for educated carp to see. This is especially advantageous in clear-water fisheries like gravel pits or mature estate lakes. If you can make the last few inches of your rig disappear it could remove the final hurdle to tricking a cautious fish.

Fluorocarbon is also very stiff, which can make it hard for carp to spit out the hookbait once they've picked it up. It can also cope with rubbing through weed, lilies or branches without snapping.

Types of hook

There's a huge range of hooks to pick from.

There are dozens of hook patterns available, and manufacturers like Korda, Fox, Nash, E-S-P, Solar and Gardner make reliable versions in a host of different shapes. Rather than looking at particular brands of hook the big picture above shows the general shapes that many manufacturers use, and we'll explain what the differences are along with when and where you should use them.

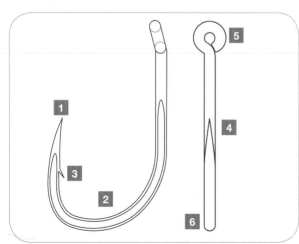

First, the picture shows the anatomy of a hook, so that we can be clear on the terminology applied to their design:

1 **Point** – The sharp bit! Can be straight or in-turned towards the shank.
2 **Gape** – The width between the hook point and the shank of the hook. Some are narrow, others are much wider.
3 **Barb** – The optional appendage on the back of the hook point that's designed to give the hook a firmer hold. Barbless hooks are now available in most patterns, as some fisheries insist on their use since they're easier to remove.
4 **Shank** – The backbone of the hook. Most are straight, but some are curved. The length can also vary, with some short and others very long.
5 **Eye** – The junction point between hook and hooklink. Can be in-turned (pointing towards the point), straight, or out-turned (pointing away from point).
6 **Gauge** – Carp hooks are all made of relatively thick, strong wire, but not all are the same. Some are made with extra-strong wire to cope with big fish or snaggy situations while others are of lighter weight for surface-fishing or open-water situations.

Wide gape

One of the most popular patterns, these are relatively short-shanked hooks with a wide gape and usually an in-sweeping point. This hook pattern is best used when legering with a bait hard on the lake bed. The wide gape is designed to increase the chance of pricking a fish sucking in your bait, while the in-turned point reduces how many hook points get damaged when they land on a hard, gravelly lake bed. They also produce a firm hook hold. The in-turned point is designed to turn over the hook to prick the inside of a carp's mouth when it picks up your bait.

Curve shank

This is another hugely popular modern shape of hook, with a gentle curve on the shank. It's a shape that's good at turning the hook to prick a fish sucking up your bait and also produces very reliable hook holds. This is a general-purpose pattern that's good both for baits legered on the bottom and for buoyant baits that are popped-up an inch or two off the lake bed, as the bait can be placed in a good position on the curved shank.

Long shank

A hook pattern that's designed to make it hard for fish to eject a bait they've sucked up. It's also good for producing deep and super-secure holds, which means you land the vast majority of the fish you hook. Can be used for pop-ups, although they're generally used mostly for baits legered hard on the bottom.

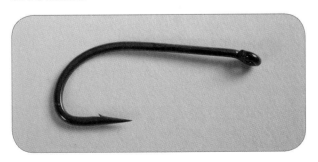

Floater

Although many companies don't produce hooks specifically for fishing on the surface there are a few, such as Korda's Mixa range, that are purpose-made, while the others shown here are simply smaller and lighter-weight hooks that don't weigh down the floating bait. It's essential you use a lighter wire gauge and go for smaller size hooks like 10s and 12s.

Chod

This shape of hook is made for a specific rig that we'll detail in Chapter 5. Because of the way a chod rig works this is a short-shanked, wide gape hook with an out-turned eye that's purpose-made for use with a pop-up boilie set-up on a very short hooklink. We'll explain later how to tie a chod rig, but there are now so many hooks on the market that are made specifically for this rig that it deserves a category of its own.

And what about the size?

Matching the size of your hook with the size of your hookbait is an essential rig-making skill. Carp often inspect baits before they confidently eat them, and a small bait that doesn't behave like any of the free offerings because it's weighed down by a big, heavy hook is likely to be refused. On the flipside, a really small hook hidden behind a big bait is far less likely to prick a fish that sucks it up.

Also bear in mind that there's little consistency in the respective sizes of hooks. A size 6 from one manufacturer may be significantly bigger or smaller than a size 6 from another company, so the guide below can only provide a rough approximation. To add further confusion some companies have introduced odd-numbered hook sizes 5, 7, 9 and 11, so you have more options to tinker with your hook in relation to the bait.

This guide gives you a general idea of how to match bait and hook sizes:

- **Size 4** – This is the biggest hook size you're ever likely to use for carp fishing and is saved for big baits like a 20mm boilie or two 18mm baits.
- **Size 6** – Probably the most popular size of hook and perfect for an 18mm hookbait or two 16mm baits.
- **Size 8** – Another hugely popular size that's good for a 14–16mm bait or larger particle baits like tiger nuts.
- **Size 10** – Smaller and therefore better for 12–14mm boilies/pellets and small tiger nuts.

Beating tangles

In the rig-making section later on you'll see a number of different mechanisms to avoid tangles. Many of the rig kits you'll see include components that are specifically made to stop your rig tangling when it's cast out or retrieved. So what are these tangle busters, and how do they work?

Anti-tangle tube

This is the original way to avoid tangles. It utilises slightly stiff hollow tubing with a 0.75mm bore. A length of this tubing at least 2in (5cm) longer than the hooklink is threaded up the mainline above the hooklink. This effectively stiffens the line and stops the hooklink wrapping round it in flight. Like many rig components it's available in many colours, so you can camouflage it to suit the lake bed.

Leadcore

This heavy two-piece material features a lead wire core covered in a woven braid sheath. Principally designed to pin the line to the bottom and hide it away from spooky fish, it has the added benefit of acting like a stiff boom that's very difficult to tangle. In this book we'll only show ready-tied leadcore leaders, as they offer good value, are very well tied and, most importantly, are supplied with beads that'll safely pull off the leadcore should the line snap. This prevents a hooked fish being tethered to a snapped line. Check before you use a leadcore leader, as a good number of fisheries ban their use because they can all too easily tether a hooked fish if they're poorly tied.

Anti-tangle tubing serves several purposes. As its name suggests, it helps prevent the hooklink tangling with the mainline on the cast, and it also helps protect the flanks of the fish as you play it.

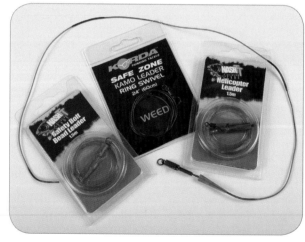

Camo leader

A relatively recent innovation, the camo leader has become hugely popular, and is truly superb. This is actually my preferred anti-tangle device and I use one for much of my fishing. Several manufacturers produce these stiff leaders, and although they all differ slightly they're based on a core of extra-strong line that's coated in plastic to stiffen it. Nash's Diffusion leaders are one example, while Korda's Hybrid leader system has small blobs of tungsten covered by the plastic so that it sinks like a brick.

Other rig components

Here's a quick list of the other key rig components and what they're used for.

Swivels

Bigger-barrel swivels are used to attach hooklinks to mainline. The rolling action of the swivel stops the line twisting,

which also avoids tangles. Smaller swivels can be used to attach baits to hooks.

Silicone and shrink tubing

This fine 0.5mm or 0.75mm soft rubber tubing is designed to pin the hair rig to the back of the hook, keeping the rig in the correct shape. Shrink tube is used in the same way, but is held over steaming water to cause it to contract and trap the hair rig in position.

Rig rings and bait floss

Small stainless steel rings that are used to present a bait tight to the back of a hook,

often using a fine floss thread to tie the hookbait to the ring.

Braid blades

Ordinary scissors are of little use for rig tying, especially when you're cutting super-strong braided lines. These thin-bladed scissors are devilishly sharp.

Flying backlead

A small leger weight running on your mainline between the rig and the rod. Designed to sink your line and keep it out of the sight of wary fish.

Quick-change clips and loops

Useful for connecting hooklinks to the rest of the rig and to allow hooklinks to be quickly clipped on to and unclipped from the rig.

Sleeves

Small lengths of thin tubing positioned at the top of the hooklink to stop tangles.

So, now that we've looked at what tackle you should use and what you should make rigs out of, it's time to do the essential bit and draw it all together as we make the last few inches of line that hooks the fish. It's time to make your hooklink…

33

CHAPTER 4 Carp Fishing Manual
TYING A HOOKLINK

You now have the grounding needed to start along the road to becoming a successful carp angler – you understand the fish itself and you know the key pieces of kit you need in order to catch them. Now we move on to the business end of carp fishing, tying the end tackle that will hook and land the fish of your dreams.

The last few inches of your rig – the line and hook to which the bait is attached – is known as the hooklink or hooklength, and is of huge importance to your success or failure. In this chapter I'll tell you how to tie hooklinks. I'll cover the main materials (braid, coated braid, fluorocarbon and stiff filament) and describe a range of methods for tying hooklinks from them.

Although they all have subtle differences, take note of the fundamental similarity between all the hooklinks that I'll show you – the fact that the bait is NOT actually attached to the hook.

In every case it's fixed to a piece of line hanging below the hook, known as a hair rig (so called because the first versions were tied with human hair). This method of tying a hooklink is the dominant tactic in modern carp fishing.

If you think back to the chapter detailing the carp's behaviour you'll remember that carp suck up their food like a hoover; they don't pick up bait in their lips. This is why leaving the hook bare gives you such an advantage, as it increases the likelihood of pricking a carp sucking up your bait.

The hair rig is king, and in this chapter we'll see how to tie a number of variations that will cover 99% of carp-fishing situations.

So let's have a look at some hooklinks that will serve you well, but before we do, one thought. You can have the best gear in the world, but one poor knot in the system and it's all for nothing. It's really important that you tie each knot carefully and test it fully. If you're not sure of any of the knots I mention in the following chapters, go to the special knots section (pages 182 to 186) after chapter 14, where I take a look at all the knots I mention in the manual.

So let's tie some hooklinks!

Tying a basic braided hooklink

This is a great general-purpose hooklink that can be used with baits lying on the lake bed or popped-up an inch or two off the deck. Soft, supple and very thin, the big advantage this rig delivers is that it allows the hookbait to behave

exactly like free offerings. Personally, it's the rig I use for most of my fishing on lakes, whether the lake bed is silty, muddy or gravelly. It's also good with PVA bags when kept short (see Chapter 10).

1 The components: soft braid, size 8 swivel or a Korda Link Loop, hook, anti-tangle sleeve, baiting needle, boilie stops and a knot-puller. My two favourite braids are Korda's 18lb weed green Supernatural and ESP's Camo Sink Link. These are very limp, low-diameter lines that blend into the beds of most lakes. Cut off 15in.

2 Form a small loop in the end of the braid using a basic overhand knot.

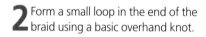

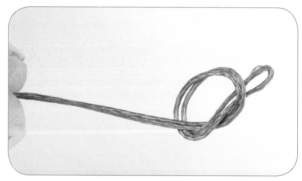

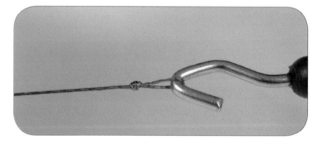

3 Use the knot-puller to pull it tight.

4 Push your chosen bait on to your baiting needle, hook the needle into your loop and transfer the bait on to the braid.

5 Take a boilie stop and place it into the loop, then bring the bait back to it, so that it's all held in place.

The next stages involve tying what's called a 'no-knot', so called because technically there's no actual knot; but don't panic – it's a very secure system of attaching a hook to a hooklength.

6 Take your braid and thread it through your chosen hook, making sure you thread from the outside of the bend inwards.

7 Pull all the braid through until the bait is hanging just below the bend of the hook.

Now let's turn our attention to the other end of the hooklength. For a short hooklength – for use in a PVA bag, for example – it's now simply a case of tying a swivel or link loop on the end. For longer braid hooklengths it's a good idea to include an anti-tangle sleeve.

8 Trap the braid to the bend of the hook and carefully whip eight turns down the hook shank, then two back over the other turns. Thread the end of the braid back through the hook eye, again from the back to the front.

9 You now have the completed no-knot tied. The knotless knot produces an angled position that's good for pricking fish sucking up the bait.

10 Slide a Korda silicone sleeve or anti-tangle sleeve down the hooklink – these soft pieces of tubing help avoid tangles on the cast.

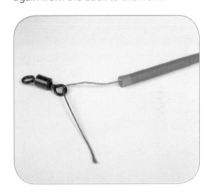

11 Using the very reliable grinner knot (see knots section), attach your swivel or link loop. Bring the sleeving back up to the swivel knot, then push it over to hold it in place.

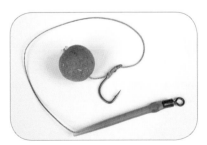

12 For most situations a hooklink of 6in to 9in is ideal.

13 Secure the hooklink on a rig board. This one fits inside the Korum ITM tackle box, a really neat storage system.

Tying a basic coated braid hooklink

The largest potential problem with using small-diameter soft braids is that they can be prone to tangling on the cast. This is probably the main reason why coated braids have become so popular in recent years.

With a soft braid at the core and a plastic coating to stiffen it, this line gives you the potential to tie a rig that enjoys the best of both materials. Here's how you tie a coated braid rig that resists tangles and yet still gives the hookbait maximum movement. There are lots of coated braids and they're all very good, but I prefer the softer-coated versions, such as Korda N-Trap Soft.

1 The components – coated braid, size 8 swivel or Korda Link Loop, hook, knot-puller, silicone/anti-tangle sleeves, a baiting needle and boilie stops.

2 Cut off 12in of hooklink material and use a stripping tool to remove the last 5in of plastic coating and expose the soft braid core.

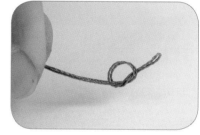

3 Tie a loop in the end of the soft braid as per the braided hooklink. This will give the hookbait natural movement.

4 As for the braided hooklink, attach your chosen hookbait to the braid and then no-knot it to the hook.

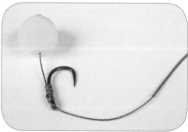

5 By stripping the plastic coating off the braid you've been left with a soft hair and 2in of exposed braid above the hook.

6 The soft braid is vital in giving the bait mounted on the hair loop a lot of movement that mimics how the free offerings will move. At the other end, use a well-lubricated grinner knot to attach a swivel or link loop.

7 The coated upper section of the hooklink is stiffer and therefore much less likely to tangle than a hooklink tied entirely out of soft braid.

8 One of the best uses of stripped coated braid is to present a pop-up boilie hookbait. Attach a lump of tungsten putty or a split shot to the bottom of the coating.

9 With a buoyant pop-up boilie on the hair, drop the bait in a small tub of water to test that the weight you've added is enough to anchor it.

10 This is the perfect multi-purpose hooklink material. Flexible yet stiff, strong yet soft, it's probably the most popular type of hooklength.

The KD rig variation

Both the pure braid and coated braid hooklinks we've tied made use of the standard knotless knot, which sees the hair rig formed from a continuation of the hooklink which is then whipped to the hook. This set-up is simple to master, is very efficient and catches a lot of carp. However, a slight variation on the rig that's growing in popularity is called the KD rig, named after its innovator, top carp angler Kenny Dorset.

The sequence below shows how you tweak the knotless knot to produce a hook that sits at a sharper angle. It's a shape that can produce more and better hook holds. Here's how you tie it.

1 As for braid, cut off the desired length – in this case of Korda Super Natural – and tie a small loop in the end.

2 Thread the braid through the back of the hook eye and position the end of the loop where you want it to sit for the size of bait you're using.

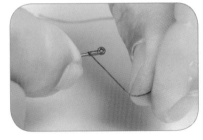

3 Whip down the shank two or three turns, trapping the line against the hook.

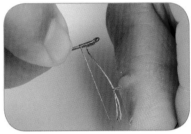

4 Fold the hair loop forward and whip the braid down the shank a further five or six times below the hair.

5 Thread the braid through the hook eye as before and pull tight. The hair now juts out of the hook at an angle. Attach a hookbait and you're in business. Note the difference between the KD-rigged bait and the standard knotless knotted bait. The angle the hook sits at can prove better at pricking wary fish that suck and blow at rigs to check whether or not they're safe.

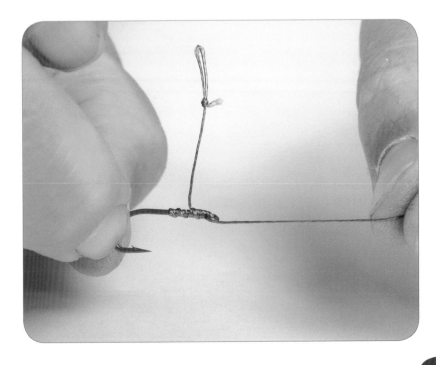

Tying a nylon/fluorocarbon hooklink

Before braid and coated braids came along nylon monofilament was the standard hooklink material, but it drifted out of fashion as the newer materials were introduced. However, a nylon line is still a good hooklink material, especially if you're casting a long way when you're fishing a bait lying on the lake bed, as its relative stiffness means it's resistant to tangles. It's also inconspicuous, so it's good at catching wary carp. It's also very cheap.

New life has been breathed into this set-up by the advent of fluorocarbon. As explained in the previous chapter, this line is stiffer than ordinary nylon so it's even more resistant to tangles; it also has the same refractive index as water – in angler's language this means it virtually disappears when it's cast into the lake!

This makes it a good choice when fishing in clear-water pools, and it's also used by a hardcore of anglers when they fish at long range, as it's so good at avoiding tangles. Here's how you tie a fluorocarbon hooklink.

1 The components – a modern softer version of fluorocarbon such as Korda's IQ2 or E-S-P Ghost soft, a size 8 or 9 curved shank hook such as an E-S-P Curve Shank, Nash Fang, Korda ring swivel, and for the advanced version some fine hair braid.

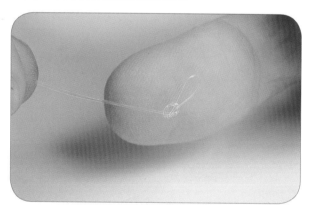

2 Let's start with the easiest and most basic version. Cut off 12–15in of line, thread it through the eye of the hook, then bend it back on itself and thread it back through the hook eye. As in previous cases, start by tying a small loop at the end.

3 Thread on your chosen bait, boilie-stop it in place and then thread it on to the hook, remembering to come from the back direction. Adjust the distance so the bait is just below the hook bend.

4 No-knot in place … job done!

This basic system will catch you fish, but because of the stiffness of the nylon/fluorocarbon the hookbait can't move freely, so some anglers worry that fish will be lost or not hooked at all. A better system involves making the hair from a more flexible material. This is my preferred option.

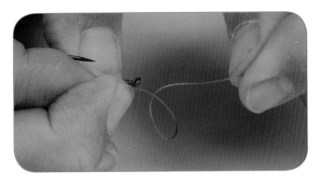

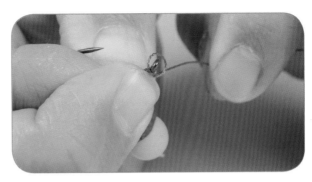

5 Cut off about 8in of a fine hair braid (I like Kryston Hair Braid). Treat it as a short braid hooklength by tying a small loop and putting your chosen bait on it. Go through the stages of no-knotting it to the hook shank, but for the final stage instead of threading it back through the hook eye, twist it to form a loop and pass it over the hook eye.

6 Repeat this process to form a second loop over the hook eye. Pull it tight.

7 Trim off the spare braid.

8 You now have your flexible hair firmly tied to the hook.

9 Cut off 12in of your nylon/fluorocarbon and Palomar it to the hook (see knots section).

10 Trim off the spare nylon/fluorocarbon.

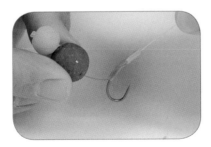

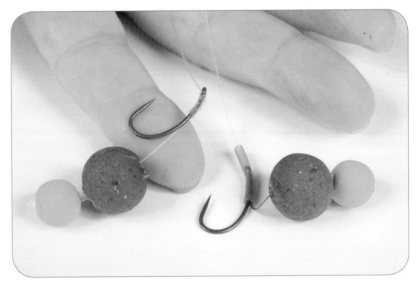

11 Cut off a 1cm length of 0.5mm silicone tube or shrink tube and thread it on to the nylon/fluorocarbon. Pull it down over the two knots.

12 Just comparing the two versions will help you understand why perfecting the tying of the advanced version will be worth the effort – the extra movement of the bait really can make the difference between catching or not!

13 Use a Palomar knot to attach a link loop or swivel. Start with a hooklink 8in long, but experiment with longer or shorter hooklinks and decide which performs best.

Tying the combi rig

In the previous six pages we've looked at the most popular and productive styles of hooklink construction. It's now time to examine slightly more advanced set-ups. But don't make the mistake of thinking that 'advanced' always means 'better' – the basic braid or coated braid hooklinks I've detailed are amongst the most successful hooklengths of all time, and will continue to catch lots of carp for ever!

However, there are times when a rig that presents a bait somewhat differently can score, and this is especially the case on busy day-ticket waters where the fish face a lot of angling pressure and get adept at avoiding capture on the types of hooklink that they confront regularly. Under such circumstances doing something just a little bit out of the ordinary can sometimes make the difference between

catching and not, and one of the smartest ways to present a hookbait is by using a combi rig.

For this two-piece hooklink, where stiff fluorocarbon and soft braid are joined together, we'll be using an Albright knot. My preference is to have the stiffer material forming the longer top section of the hooklink and a shorter piece of soft braid near the hook on the bottom of the link. Some anglers reverse this relationship, but I believe the way it's shown here gives the finished rig the best properties of both line materials.

The fluorocarbon is almost invisible in water, so it's difficult for wary carp to spot, and because it's very stiff it's exceptionally good at resisting tangles. The braid then gives the final few inches of the rig a huge degree of movement to present the bait naturally.

1 You'll need your chosen braid, your chosen fluorocarbon, a hook, plus for a neat little tweak at the end some Korda sinkers.

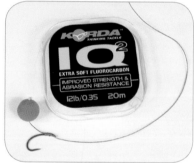

2 Cut off about 8in of braid and make it up as you would a normal braid hooklength.

3 Get a length of strong fluorocarbon such as E-S-P Ghost or Korda IQ2, double it back on itself to create a loop and thread the braid through it.

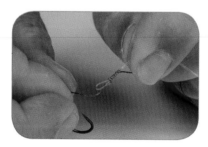

4 Whip eight turns of braid down the fluorocarbon loop.

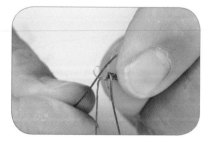

5 Then whip six more turns of braid back towards the hook. Pass the end of the braid through the end of the loop.

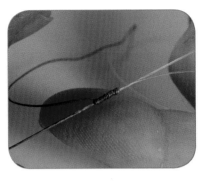

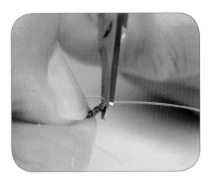

6 Moisten the knot and tease it tight, whipping the two lines together.

7 Trim off the spare fluorocarbon tight to the knot.

8 The spare braid slightly longer, leaving a short tag.

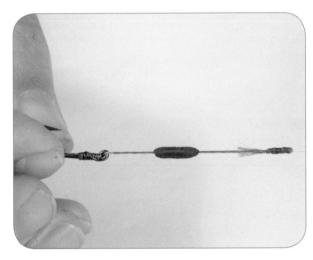

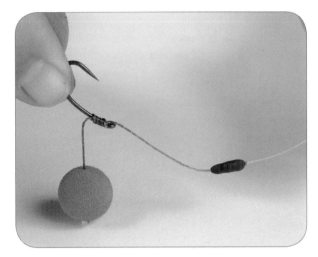

9 Now for the clever bit! Wet the knot, then slide a large Korda sinker down the fluorocarbon and over the knot, and bring it back over the knot so that it covers and protects the knot in use. The really clever bit is that this sinker will also help pull the hook downwards into the fish's bottom lip, making it a very efficient rig for pricking wary fish.

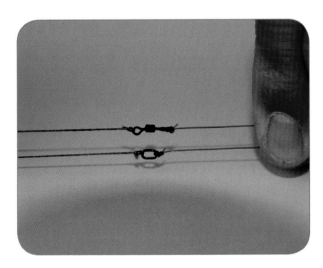

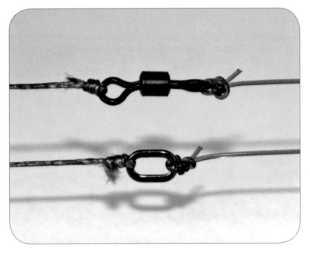

Note: If you find this knot difficult, an alternative to whipping the two lines together is to use a tiny metal rig ring or micro swivel as a connection. Grinner knot the braid to the ring or swivel and Palomar knot the fluorocarbon to the ring or swivel.

Tying a multi rig

This is an advanced version of the coated braid rig and was the brainchild of rig mastermind Mick Kavanagh. It might look a bit weird, as the hook isn't actually tied to the end of the line, but it's a set-up that's proven its credentials in recent years and has become a recognised set-up.

It works by creating an acute hooking angle, and fish have real trouble ejecting the bait once they've sucked it in. It has an excellent hook-up ratio.

Another reason why this rig has proved so popular is that it's good with both bottom and pop-up baits. It's a general-purpose rig that can be used on almost every carp water. Here's how you tie it, in this case as a pop-up presentation.

1 The components – 20lb Korda N-trap coated braid, a mini Korda ring swivel, a size 8–10 hook with an out-turned eye like an E-S-P Stiff Rigger MK2, a Fox SR Arma Point or a Korda Mixa, and some hair braid.

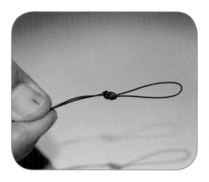
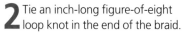

2 Tie an inch-long figure-of-eight loop knot in the end of the braid.

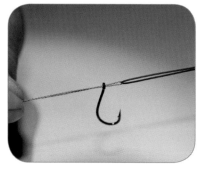

3 Pull the loop through the eye of the hook (front to back). It's generally easier to use a loop of thin braid to help get the thicker loop through the hook eye.

4 Thread the mini swivel on to the loop.

5 Run the hook and swivel down to the knot. Check there are no twists in the loop, then pass the end of the loop over the hook point to secure the hook to the braid, trapping the mini swivel in a small D loop in the process.

6 Thread a length of hair braid through the mini swivel and double it up. Use a boilie needle to bring both ends through your bait, then tie the ends off around a boilie stop.

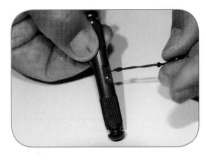

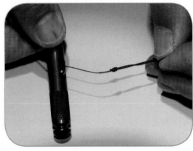

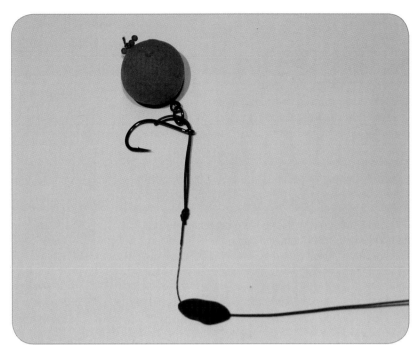

7 Use a stripper tool to remove a short length of the outer coating, starting at the loop knot. Exposing the soft braid will help to give the hookbait natural movement. If using a pop-up, how much you remove will determine how far off the bottom your bait will sit.

8 If using a pop-up, mould a small amount of tungsten putty around the end of the uncoated braid. Use just enough to make the pop-up sink slowly.

You've now got a great pop-up presentation where the hook sits at a very acute angle, which is a great position to nick a carp sucking in the bait. The clever bit about the multi rig is that the bait can be changed, as can the hook if the point gets blunted. Just open up the D, push the loop back over the hook point and replace the hook. You can also use this rig with bottom baits. Swap the hook for a long shank or similar pattern and attach a stainless rig ring on the D loop.

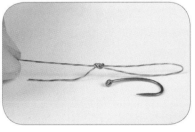

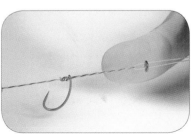

Tying a chod hooklink

We'll be looking at the chod rig in the next chapter (when we look at the various leger systems to which you can attach your hooklink), but in a nutshell the chod hooklink is a 4in curved hooklength of stiff filament line designed to be used with buoyant pop-up hookbaits that will sit up on weedy, silty or debris-covered lake beds, commonly called 'chod' – whence the name of the rig.

Made famous by top-flight carpers like Terry Hearn and Nigel Sharp, this rig has achieved cult status over recent years and is now in widespread use. Several companies such as Korda and ESP produce excellent ready-tied chod rig hooklengths.

If you wish to tie your own, here's how you tie the key part of the finished rig, the short hooklink itself.

1 The components – a size 8 Korda Choddy or Fox SR or E-S-P Stiff Rigger hook, Korda Mouthtrap or E-S-P Stiff Rigger or Fox Rigidity filament line, mini size 11 ring swivels and a mini rig ring.

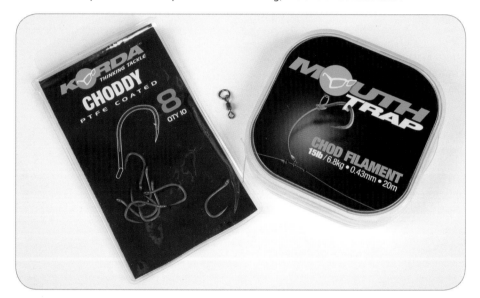

2 Cut off a length of Mouthtrap and grinner knot it to the ring of the ring swivel. Two or three turns on the knot will be sufficient as the line is so stiff. For security you can use a lighter to 'blob' the tag end.

Basically we're now going to use a whipping knot (also called a Snell knot) to attach the hook to the Mouthtrap.

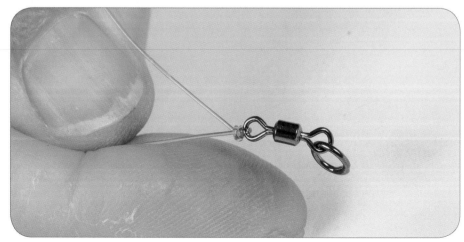

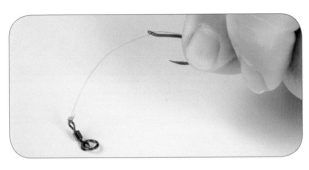

3 Thread the line through the front of the hook, taking care to make sure the natural curve in the line follows the curve of the hook.

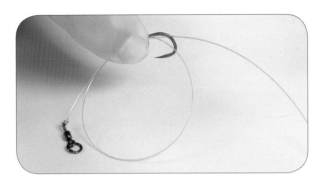

4 Fold it back to form a loop.

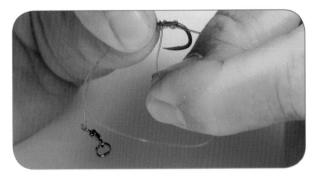

5 Holding the loop of filament, whip up the line three or four times, trapping the loop.

6 Keep hold of the whipping to stop it unravelling as you pull the tag end so that the spare loop disappears. Ease the knot tight to the shank and then ease it up to the eye.

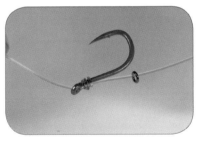

7 Slide a rig ring on to the tag end of the stiff filament.

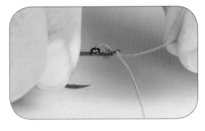

8 Bend it through the hook eye and pull the tag so that a small 'D' shape of line is formed on the back of the hook.

9 Cut off the spare tag, leaving approximately 5mm.

10 Burn the tag end of line with a low lighter flame, melting it to form a blob.

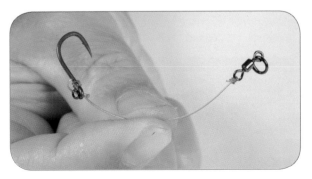

11 The blob locks the D hair, trapping the ring in the small loop on the back of the hook. Pull the hooklink tightly over the end of your finger to curve it.

Tying a Withy Pool rig

This advanced rig has a hook set-up that looks bizarre but has delivered great results over the years, and has a band of disciples who believe it's one of the most effective ways to catch carp on buoyant pop-up boilies. The reason for its success lies in the aggressive angle at which the hook sits, in a perfect position directly below the bait – any fish that mouths the bait is likely to get pricked by the hook.

Developed at Bedfordshire's Withy Pool, the rig was

designed to trick clued-up carp that had become good at avoiding traditional set-ups. It worked brilliantly, and since then the popularity of the rig has grown. It used to be really tricky to tie, but the Fox adaptor shown here has made it much simpler. Here's how you tie up a Withy Pool rig the easy way...

1 The components – a coated braid such as Fox Coretex or Korda Semi Stiff N Trap, a curved shank hook like a Fox SSC, Korda Kaptor Kurve or E-S-P Curve Shanx, mini ring swivels, bait floss/hair braid, a small rubber rig stop and a Fox Withy Pool adaptor.

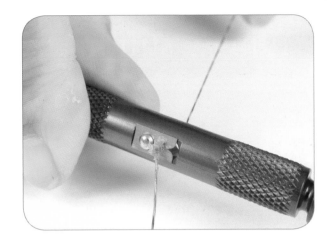

2 Snip off 12in of coated braid and strip off the last 3in.

3 Tie the hook on with a grinner knot.

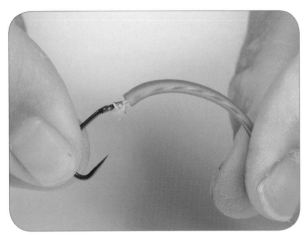

4 Thread the Withy Pool adaptor on to the braid and slide it over the hook eye. The tiny serrations at the end of the tubing should be at the opposite end to the hook.

5 Thread the mini ring swivel on to the hook, followed by the tiny rubber rig stop bead so that the ring is trapped between the bead and the hook eye.

6 Mould enough rig putty, such as Nash Cling-On, round the special ridges at the end of the adaptor – this anchors the bait – and the finished set-up is ready to be cast out. Note how the last few inches of line sit like a claw primed to prick a feeding fish.

7 It's just a matter of attaching your bait to the ring on the small swivel and adjusting the amount of putty to make sure the bait sits right. (See 'Mounting a bait' on page 52.)

Tying a stiff hinge rig

This is an unusual and advanced two-piece hooklink that's ideal for presenting pop-up hookbaits an inch or two off the lake bed. It's primarily used on weedy waters where it's easy for your hookbait either to become buried in debris littering the bottom or to get snagged on strands of weed as it sinks.

Various materials can be used for tying it. You can have a long, stiff upper section and a short, stiff lower piece – this produces a rig that's highly resistant to tangles and is excellent for fishing in heavy weed. Alternatively you can use the variant shown here in which coated braid forms the longer top part of the link while the lower piece is made from exceptionally stiff filament line. This is still good at resisting tangles and is one of the best hooklinks for use in weedy waters.

If weed is giving you nightmares – as it does for many newcomers to carp fishing – then a rig incorporating a stiff hinge hooklink is a great starting point.

So, let's look at how the hinge rig is tied.

1 The components – 20lb E-S-P Stiff Filament/Fox Rigidity/ Korda Mouthtrap, Korda N-Trap coated braid, size 11 ring swivel, rig ring, link loop and tungsten putty such as Korda Dark Matter or Nash Cling-on.

2 Follow the step-by-step for tying a chod hooklink (page 46-57) to produce a 1–3in length of super-stiff line. This will form the lower section of the hooklink. Tying such a short link is fiddly, so it's worth spending time to master it.

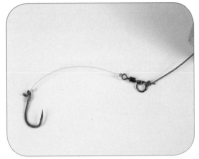

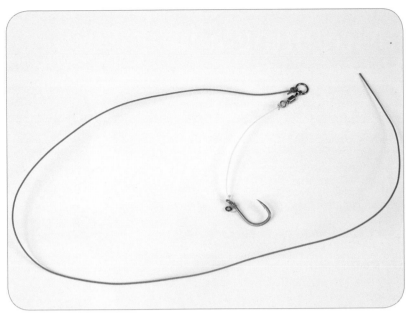

3 Now tie the longer section of the link. Use a grinner or Palomar knot to attach 10in of 20lb Korda N-Trap to the ring on the mini ring swivel.

4 Use the same grinner or Palomar knot to attach the link clip at the other end.

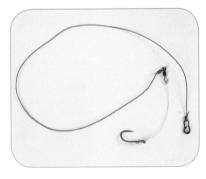

5 You now have a completed stiff hinge rig.

6 A pop-up can be added in exactly the same way as you did with the Withy Pool rig.

7 Counterbalance the pop-up with a small amount of tungsten putty moulded around the ring on the ring swivel, but be careful to make sure it doesn't restrict the movement of the swivel.

8 The stiff hinge rig can be used with both pop-ups and bottom baits.

9 It can also be used with a variety of lead systems depending on what attachment system you use on the end of the N-Trap.

Mounting a bait

2 Push the needle through the bait.

3 Hook into the loop on the rig's hair.

Thread it on

The simplest way to attach a bait to a hair rig loop is to pierce it with a sharp baiting needle, thread it on to the loop and lock it in place with a boilie stop. It's quick, simple and allows a range of different baits to be loaded on to the rig. Here's how you do it.

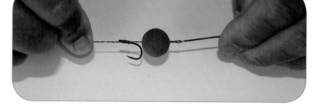

4 Transfer the boilie.

1 You need a baiting needle and a boilie stop. There's a range of baiting needles available – pick a very sharp needle that punctures the bait easily, creates a small hole in it and doesn't split the bait. Probably the best general-purpose variety is the latch needle, but the fine point of the braid needle makes a smaller hole in the bait.

5 Locate the boilie stop in the loop. Don't worry about matching colour etc.

6 Pull the bait into position.

Screw it on

Every now and again a little rig product comes along that's simple and cheap but brilliant. The ACE pop-up peg is one of these little gems. Tied on to the end of your line when you tie the hooklink, this tiny screw can be turned easily into a range of baits – you don't have to limit its use to pop-up boilies. The bait butts up tightly against the wide lip of the screw to effectively self-seal the hole it creates. The peg grips the bait surprisingly tightly so it can't be cast off on the cast. Here's how you use it.

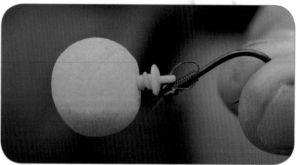

1 The tiny plastic screw is tied on the end of the hooklink, or it can be trapped inside the D-loop created on many set-ups.

2 The bait is simply screwed on to the peg. When you want to re-bait just break the bait off and screw on a new one. Designed for attaching pop-up boilies to your rig, there's no reason why it can't be used with baits like Peperami, tiger nuts or sinking boilies.

Tie it on

This is a technique used to loop soft floss tightly round a pop-up bait before the floss is tied to a rig attached to the end of the hooklink.

The reason for choosing this method of attaching the hookbait to the hooklink is to avoid piercing it. This stops water invading the bait and reducing its buoyancy, which in turn makes precise balancing and anchoring of the bait very easy, as you can test it in the margins of the lake when you mount it on the rig, safe in the knowledge that its buoyancy won't change much over the time it spends in the water.

This is especially useful when you use pop-up baits made with a cork ball in the centre (see Chapter 6), as it prevents water ingress and stops the buoyancy of the bait changing. Here's how you tie on a bait.

1 Take a short length of bait floss and form a sliding loop in it.

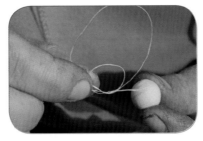

2 Place the loop over the hookbait and tighten the loop around it to grip the boilie.

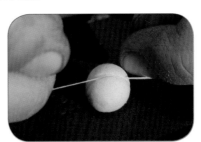

3 Tie a couple more overhand knots to secure the knot and grip the bait tightly enough for casting.

4 Pass one tag end through the metal ring found on various chod/hinge rigs and tie three overhand knots to secure it.

5 Cut the loose end of floss off, leaving about 5mm.

6 Carefully burn the tag ends to 'blob' the line and prevent it unravelling.

Finishing off the rig

You now know all about the fish you want to catch, the items of essential tackle you need and how to tie the last few inches of the rig that make up the hooklink – in other words, the business end of your rig. Now it's time to complete your rig by making the part that gives it the weight it needs to cast bait where you want it and to hook a fish that picks up your bait.

There are countless ways to attach a leger weight to a rig, and many experienced carpers combine different rig components to engineer their own unique set-ups. Indeed, it's the proliferation of rig-making products to service such skills that creates much of the confusion that exists among novice carp anglers. What on earth are all those rings, beads, swivels and bits of plastic needed for? If you get baffled,

don't worry about it – you're not alone. I often scratch my head too, and I've been a carper for 25 years!

In the next chapter I'll cut through this jungle of confusion by detailing six basic leger systems that can be easily pieced together and used with the hooklinks just described to complete your set-up. In each case I've made up the rigs using components that are readily available in many tackle shops. They've been tested, carefully designed, and in most cases can be bought as ready-to-go 'systems' in a pack that contains everything you need to complete the rig.

Making things simple but efficient is what this manual is all about. The next chapter shows you how to complete your rigs and includes detailed full-page diagrams that show you how they work underwater.

COMPLETING THE BUSINESS END

I finished Chapter 4 by reminding you that this Manual is all about making things simple – which isn't something you always associate with carp angling and carp anglers. Now it's time to get down to the six basic rig systems that you can chose from and how to assemble them. The systems described are:

■ The lead clip
■ The running leger
■ The inline and inline drop-off
■ The helicopter
■ The chod
■ The zig (anchored)

All six are proven fish catchers, but the trick is to know which one to use in any given situation. I'll try to give you some help as the chapter progresses.

The lead clip

How to set up the lead clip

The lead clip is probably the most popular leger set-up of the modern era. For over a decade it has been the most frequently used method of attaching the lead weight to the line. The reasons for this popularity aren't difficult to understand. Not only is the clip easy to use and incorporate into a rig but it's also a very safe way to attach the lead and, most importantly, to dispose of the lead if it snags. For example, if the leger snags in thick weed, lilies or reeds the rubber sleeve that locks the lead in place simply slides up the line to allow the clip to open up and jettison the lead.

Shedding the leger like this massively shifts the advantage back in favour of the angler playing the fish. With no lead on the line to effectively 'tie' the rig to the snag, the chance of the line pulling clear and the fight recommencing is massively increased. By shedding the lead in weedy waters you stand a far greater chance of landing a fish.

But the lead clip isn't just for use in lakes rammed with weed. Its ease of operation and the fact that the leger can be dispensed if the fish unexpectedly snags up in an underwater obstruction means this is a hugely popular set-up on all types of water. Consequently many anglers use this set-up every time they go carp fishing.

Whether a venue is snaggy or not, this is one of the ultimate safe rigs. For example, if an angler casting a long way suffers a 'crack off' when the mainline snaps, this is a safe rig that allows the lead to be dumped if a fish picks up the bait that remains on the rig. This greatly reduces the risk of tethering the fish to an underwater snag.

There are several different ways to mount a lead clip on your reel line, and here we show all of the main techniques.

Lead clip on anti-tangle tubing

1 Anti-tangle tubing is a hollow, semi-stiff tube that can be run up the mainline. This stiffens the line, which massively reduces the risk of getting tangles on the cast. The key rule to remember is that the tubing must be around 2in longer than the hooklink you're using – in other words if your hooklength is 8in, the tubing needs to be 10in.

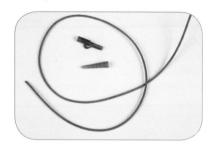

2 Firstly, you need your chosen tubing and a matching tail rubber and lead clip. It's a good idea to stay with one company for all these components, as they're designed to work together. I use Korda components.

3 Thread your mainline through the tubing, followed by the tail rubber and the lead clip itself. Before threading, cut the mainline at an angle. This makes it easier to thread down the tubing. Many anglers mistakenly lick the line to help it thread; *don't* – it sticks to the inside wall instead. Tie on your hooklength with a grinner or Palomar knot.

4 Push the swivel into the clip and pull the mainline until the swivel locks. With the Korda lead clip shown here the swivel fits with an audible 'click' so that you know it's locked.

5 Several other clips, such as the E-S-P, Avid, Solar and Nash designs, are all supplied with pegs that slot into a hole to permanently fix the swivel and clip them together. Although this may seem dangerous, as it seems to permanently fix the lead and line together, it's designed to create a solid base to help the lead eject if it snags up.

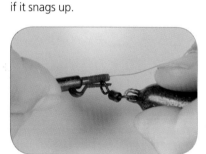

6 Clip your lead on to the lead clip.

7 Bring the tail rubber down and push over the top of the lead clip, trapping the lead in place.

8 Hold the lead clip and push the tubing into the top of the tail rubber.

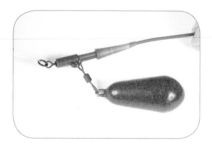

9 It's important to understand that the tail rubber is your means of adjustment. If you want the lead to eject easily when you get a run – for example when fishing in weed – hardly push the tail rubber over at all. In clear water, fishing in silt, you can afford to push it much further on and keep your lead on the take. It's all a matter of judgement.

Your lead clip system is now complete and ready to use.

There are many types of anti-tangle tubing. I much prefer to use tungsten-impregnated tubing, which is far heavier and sinks like a stone to hide the rig and make it less obtrusive. Some people hate tubing because it can be difficult to thread. Avid tubing is pre-threaded with a thin wire to make it easier to run the line through it. Run the line through the loop on the top of the tubing and pull the other end of the wire. The line is pulled through the tubing and can then be threaded through the special Avid Tube Gripper Clip. This clip holds the tubing and stops it sliding up the mainline.

Lead clip on a ready-tied leader

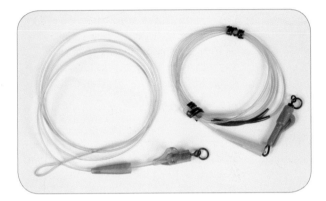

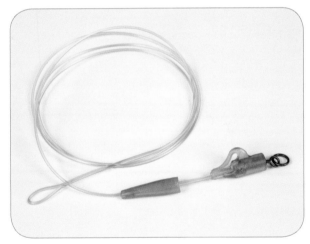

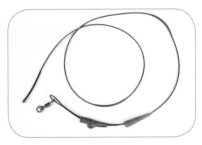

1 Several companies produce lead clip leaders that are tied to the mainline at one end with the hooklink at the other. They're made from strong fluorocarbon line coated in plastic. Nash's Diffusion leaders and Korda's Hybrid leaders are designed to sink quickly and blend into the lake bed to make the rig unobtrusive. Their stiffer leaders also resist tangles.

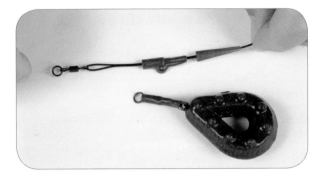

2 This is a very easy rig to set up. Slide your lead clip and tail rubber down the leader, then tie your mainline on to the top loop on the leader with a five-turn grinner knot or a Palomar knot. This is a Korda Hybrid leader finished with a loop at one end and a looped ring swivel at the other.

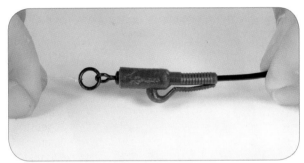

3 Pull the lead clip over the swivel as before.

4 Attach your lead as before.

5 Finally slide over the tail rubber.

Lead clip on a ready-tied leadcore leader

A similar system is available based on a leadcore leader, sometimes with a fitted lead clip.

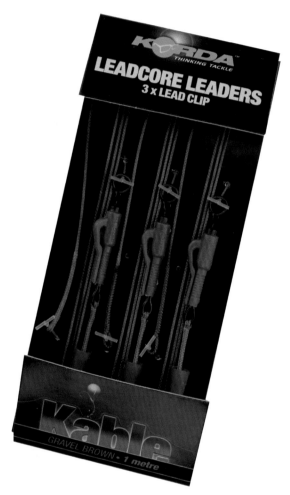

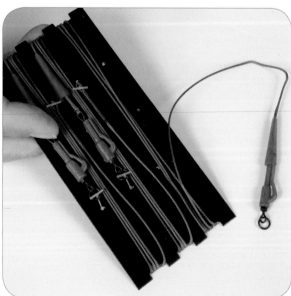

1 Unravel and pull to straighten the leadcore.

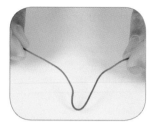 

2 Slide on your lead clip (unless already fitted) and tail rubber.

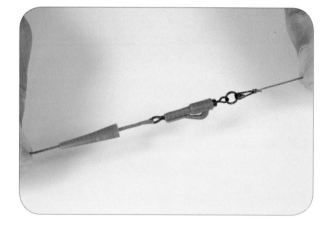

3 Tie on your leader using a grinner or Palomar knot.

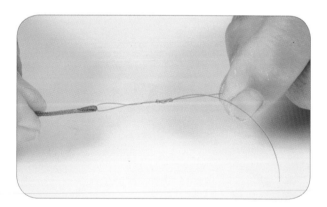

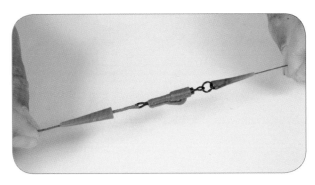

4 Clip on your hooklength and cover the clip with a short length of tubing.

5 Clip on your lead and push down tail rubber.

On some systems the lead clip is permanently fixed on to the other end of the leader, and I use a Link Loop and Kwik Link to attach the hook link – rig tied! The Korda leaders are a favourite of mine. They're loaded with tungsten to pin them down and they're so quick and easy to set up. I use them a lot.

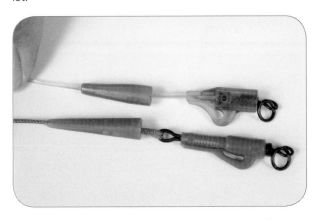

It's also important to note that there are several different designs of lead clip, some designed specifically to drop the lead more easily than others. These clips are better if you're fishing into heavy weed, but you don't need to drop leads all the time, so think carefully about your fishing situation and choose accordingly.

The lead clip – key features

There are several key points that make the use of a lead clip so popular. I think it's fair to say that lead clips of one description or another are for many carp anglers their number one choice when legering for carp.

1. It is safe for the fish, easy to set up and is also an efficient self-hooking rig that hooks fish consistently when they feed on your bait.
2. If you're looking for a rig system to use with almost any type of hook-length in almost any type of fishing situation then the lead clip will do the job.
3. Lead clip rigs featuring a leader or anti-tangle tubing are excellent at avoiding tangles. The slightly stiffer tubing or leader material stops the hook link wrapping round the mainline when it is cast.
4. Heavy, tungsten tubing or leaders impregnated with tungsten sink well to keep the rig laid out along the lake bed. Line that lies along the bottom is far less intrusive and is important if you want to avoid spooking wary fish.
5. Tubing and leaders can be colour matched to the lakebed to aid with your rig camouflage
6. Lead clip rigs are especially good in weedy or snaggy waters as the leger easily pulls off the clip if it gets snagged. This greatly improves your chances of landing a fish.
7. A lead clip and tubing/leader combination is very fish friendly as the thickness of the tubing/leader helps prevent any chance of the line catching a scale as you are playing a fish.

So, I'm a big fan of lead clips, but as with any rig system it needs carefully adjusting to make the most of it.

Remember to keep your hook link shorter than the tubing or leader material. Most pre-tied leaders will be much longer than the hook link – they're up to a metre long – but if you're making your own with anti-tangle tube make sure it is at least two inches longer than the hook link.

A typical hook link length is six to eight inches long. If you are fishing on muddy, sandy, moderately silty or gravely lakebeds, a short link like this will produce the goods. In thick weed or very deep silt, where the leger may well bury in the soft bottom, lengthening the hook link to 10, 12 or 14 inches may be an advantage.

Think about how much you push the tail rubber on. You need to think about the angling situation you are facing. In thick weed you need to 'drop the lead' on the take so the tail rubber is just pushed on very lightly, but in open water you can push it further on as it is makes no sense to lose the lead unnecessarily.

When a carp picks up the bait and straightens the hook link, the hook is pulled into it's mouth and the sudden resistance makes the fish bolt – you get a screaming take and the hook is driven home. There is no need to strike as such, just pick up the rod and engage the clutch … job done!

The running leger

How to set up the running leger

The running leger rig has come into and gone out of fashion many times, but it remains a very effective way to catch carp. The main reason for using it over other types of rig is the fact that the mainline can slide through the leger as soon as a carp picks up the hookbait. This movement feeds directly through to the bite alarm and bite indicator, giving you good bite registration.

This type of rig is popular among anglers who believe that wary fish, which have been fished for repeatedly, feed very cautiously. Instead of bolting and hooking themselves when they feel the resistance offered by the leger, these educated fish try and rid themselves of the hook: some anglers have reported seeing fish spinning on the spot until the hook is dislodged. In fact in this situation a leger that's fixed to the line – like a lead clip – is seen as a disadvantage. Not only is the sensitivity of bite indication reduced, but the leger can actually be used as an 'anvil' against which the fish can prize out the hook.

My thoughts on running legers have changed over the years and I'm beginning to use them more frequently after I watched an incredibly wary carp pick up my hookbait in gin clear water. At the time I was using the standard lead clip and leader set-up already shown in this chapter. After refusing to pick up the bait three times when it entered a margin spot I'd been baiting the fish finally made a mistake with the hookbait and sucked it up.

I was watching the whole episode from behind a bank of reeds a few feet away – I had perfect vision of what happened next, and I honestly couldn't believe it. It made me wonder how many times wary fish 'get away with it'.

As the carp went down on the hookbait I saw it disappear into the fish's mouth, and when the carp righted itself I saw the hooklink pull tight and the leger lift off the lake bed – my bite alarm never bleeped, even though there was only 6ft of line between fish and rod tip! Hovering in mid-water with the leger clearly hanging from the its mouth, the carp paused for a split second before it suddenly thrashed its head from side to side. I watched open-mouthed as the lead was thrown off the clip, and still the bite alarm didn't sound, as the line failed to twitch.

How long the fish would have carried on trying to shed the hook like this I don't know, but it was clearly a big one and I wasn't about to let it succeed in ejecting the hook. I struck the bite before the fish had moved an inch.

Interestingly the 27lb common carp I landed was one I didn't recognise, nor did an angler who has fished the lake for upwards of 20 years and knows most of the fish as well as his children!

Having watched this ultra-wary fish try to rid itself of the hook I now suspect that many of the fish that rarely get

caught in lakes simply feed in a different way, and a free-running rig that allows the line to slide through the leger might be a much better option for tricking the fish that everyone is missing.

It's only a theory, of course, and proving it will take several seasons of comparative testing, but a free-running rig is now on at least one of my rods most times that I cast out. Here are the set-ups I use.

Mounting a running leger on anti-tangle tubing

Companies such as Fox, Nash, Korda and Solar produce kits that contain all the components you need to produce a very efficient running leger rig.

Two things are essential for a running leger rig to work: you must use a heavy leger of 3oz or more, plus a run ring or swivel with a large bore to allow the line to pass easily.

The mistake often made by anglers using running legers is that they use light leads to minimise resistance – the problem is, the friction of the line sliding through the ring moves the leger. A better option is to use a heavy lead of 3oz or more that doesn't budge when the line moves through the run ring. This allows maximum indication and minimum resistance.

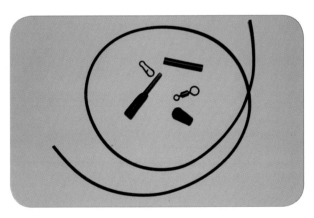

1 The components you need are anti-tangle tubing, a Big-Eye swivel, a Run Rig Rubber or Shok Bead, Lead Link clip and a silicon sleeve.

2 Cut off anti-tangle tubing longer than the hooklink and thread it on to the mainline. Cut the line at a sharp angle to help you thread it through the tubing.

3 Slide the big eye swivel onto the mainline...

4 ...followed by the Korda Run Rig rubber. This is streamlined to avoid tangles and maximise casting distance.

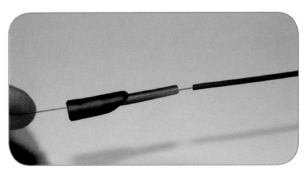

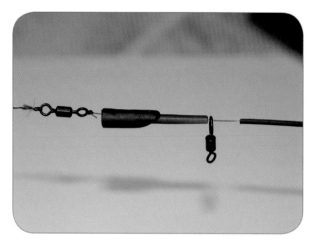

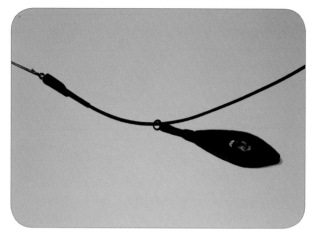

 5 Tie on your chosen hooklength.

6 Pull the Run Rig rubber over the hooklength swivel.

7 Attach the link clip to the bottom of the big eye swivel.

9 Your rig is complete and provides a very free-running system that fish find difficult to deal with, because the tubing can slide effortlessly through the heavy leger anchor. As long as you're using light weight indicators and bite alarms set to their most sensitive you'll register a slow but positive take that you can't miss – strike!

The running leger in use

As with any rig there are things to look out for to ensure the rig is functioning at its most efficient, so here's a quick tick list for the running leger.

- Use a heavy leger when fishing a running lead rig – at least 3oz or more. A dumpy pear or square shaped lead is best as it won't move or pivot like a more streamlined leger would, this helps the line slide through the leger.
- Some rules of rig making don't vary – the length of the tubing should be at least two inches longer than the hooklink to avoid tangles on the cast and retrieve.
- This type of rig is best used on firm bottomed lakes or pools with only shallow silt, if you cast a heavy lead into very deep or soft silt the leger could completely sink and what started as a running leger on the bank becomes a fixed one plugged in the silt.
- When a fish picks up the hookbait and moves off with it, the line and tubing slides through the swivel on the top of the bomb giving you the maximum amount of bite registration at the rod end. To keep resistance to a minimum, point the rod directly at the area being fished and use as light an indicator as possible.
- If you think fish are feeding warily experiment with different hook link materials and lengths. A 10 to 12 inch fluorocarbon link may be a good choice as it is impossible to see and it is more likely to remain mostly extended when the rig sinks, when a carp then picks up the bait the movement is quickly transmitted to the mainline which duly slides.

8 Attach your lead and cover the link with the silicon sleeve. This helps prevent any chance of your hooklength tangling.

The inline and inline drop-off

How to tie up inline systems

The inline system originally got its name from the fact that the lead had a hollow plastic insert running through it, through which your mainline ran, so basically everything was inline.

The basic inline system is still popular and works very well in PVA bags with very short hooklengths. The one major problem comes when you're fishing in any situation where the lead can become stuck, such as dense weed. Imagine the scenario: you've hooked a fish and it powers off. The lead clogs in weed, the swivel comes out of the lead insert and the fish keeps going, but you're effectively not playing the fish directly as the line is going back to the lead not your rod end.

So if you want to use the inline lead system in or near weed you need to modify how the lead is attached, and these days that isn't difficult, as there are several ways of making the basic inline a drop-off inline.

The basic inline system

1 You'll need your hooklength, an inline lead, tubing and a tail rubber. Start by threading the tubing on the mainline, followed by the tail rubber, then

the inline lead. Finally tie on your hooklength using a grinner knot or a Palomar knot.

2 Push the swivel into the inline's plastic insert. (Most inlines take a size 8 swivel as a firm push-fit.)

3 Push the tail rubber on the other end.

4 Pull the tubing down and push well into the tail rubber.

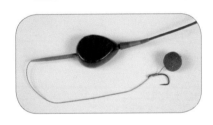

5 The rig is complete and ready to go. The picture shows the hooklength with an anti-tangle sleeve fitted. This is useful if casting without a PVA

bag etc, as it helps kick the bait away from the lead and helps prevent tangles. It isn't needed if you're using the rig in a PVA bag.

Converting your basic inline system to a drop-off inline

1 Thread your mainline through the tubing as previously, but this time thread your tail rubber

on to the tubing. Then, using a grinner knot or a Palomar knot, tie your hooklength to the mainline, but this time to the same end as the hooklength.

2 Push the loose end of the swivel into the lead's plastic insert, and the tail rubber on the other end, then adjust the tubing so it sits along the outside of the lead.

This is a simple but effective way of converting your existing inline lead to a drop-off inline, and it works very well, but some companies have taken the drop-off inline principle a stage further and designed full inline drop-off

systems. I particularly like the Avid peg system, which can also be used with their specially-designed groove leads – an excellent system.

A commercial drop-off system

The Avid inline drop-off rig is a clever little set-up. In essence it's a leger held on the line by a rubber sleeve and a special plug that fits up the rear of the lead, plus it has a groove in the lead into which the tubing slots. It cuts down tangles and, most importantly, also allows the leger to be jettisoned if it pulls into heavy weed that would have led to lost fish just a few short seasons ago.

Thanks to the plug that pulls up the rear junction and the sleeve that plugs over the front of the lead, it's a wonderfully adaptable rig that drops the main cause of lost fish if the line becomes snagged. The ability to free the line from all obstructions and still stay in contact with the fish is a brilliant tactic that can make the difference between

landing a fish and losing it in weed. If this isn't reason enough to always carry this set-up in your back pocket, there's another one: it's a cheap and easy set-up that anyone can soon tackle.

THE COMMERCIAL 'AVID' DROP-OFF SYSTEM

As the fish moves off the plug pulls out of the lead.

Once the plug is pulled out, the weight of the lead helps the lead pull out of the tail rubber and it falls free.

The Avid inline drop-off set-up (with tubing)

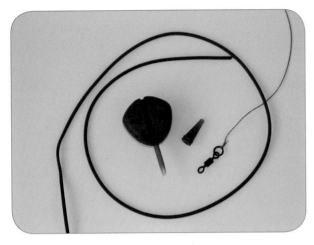

1 Avid's in-line drop-off groove system is a brilliant but easy-to-use system that's simple to get to grips with. You can use these leads with specially designed Avid components or with a standard ring swivel.

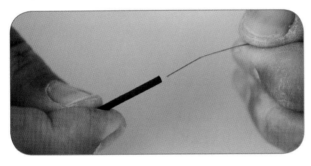

2 Thread the mainline through the tubing.

3 Thread the Avid tail rubber on to the tubing.

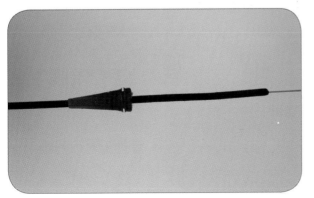

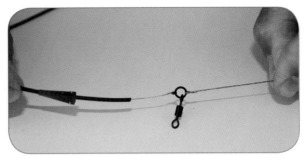

4 Tie the mainline to the ring of the hooklength ring swivel (or the Avid stem, if you're using one).

5 Plug the swivel or Avid stem into the lead insert.

6 Line up the mainline with the groove cut into the lead, and then push the tail rubber on to the insert top.

7 The finished rig – the lead easily comes off if the rig becomes snagged.

65

The Avid inline drop-off set-up (with a leader)

1 Using a grinner or Palomar knot, tie on the leader, in this case a Korda Safe Zone leader.

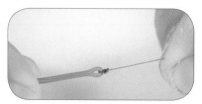

5 Cover the clip with 2cm of silicon tubing.

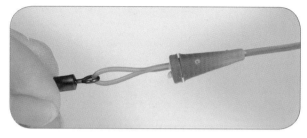

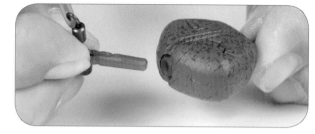

2 Thread an Avid tail rubber on to the leader.

3 Push the Avid plug on to the leader ring.

6 Push the Avid plug into the lead.

7 Line up the leader in the groove and push on the tail rubber.

4 Clip on the hooklength.

8 The finished rig – the lead easily comes off if the rig becomes snagged.

How to bag up the rig

Although I deal with PVA bags later, in Chapter 10, it's worth at this point describing possibly my most recommended use of a short inline system – in a solid PVA bag. The PVA parcel holds the rig and a mass of tiny feed items, which are parcelled up, along with the rig, and cast into a lake, often reaching long ranges that you'd normally struggle to cast.

1 Place the PVA bag loading device inside the bag, to open it up.

2 Place the rig inside the bag, with the hooklink and bait hanging down.

3 Fill the bag with tiny pellets.

4 Lower the rig on to the pellets when the bag is half-full, and top up.

5 Twist the bag and tie it off with PVA string, drawing the bag shut.

6 Pull out any slack bits of the bag and dampen them with your finger. Stick the loose flaps of dampened PVA down as they go sticky.

7 Pierce the bag with a needle to let the air escape and help the bag sink. The finished bag is then ready to be cast – a neat and simple package.

A more detailed step-by-step showing how to make bags can be found in Chapter 10.

A SOLID PVA BAG IN USE

The PVA bag is tight and firm and can be cast for miles.
   Small bags are best. Use them with heavy legers of at least 2.5oz.
   Non-water-based flavours and oils can be added to the bag to increase its attraction.

A plume of fish oil bursts out to draw fish in to feed.

If the swim is weedy the bag plunges into it, then breaks open, releasing the hookbait.

Fish are attracted to the bait and they soon suck up the hookbait.

The helicopter

How to tie a helicopter rig

This is a rig that sprung to prominence in the 1990s, when many anglers liked its anti-tangle properties and distance-casting potential. It got its name from the rotational movement of the hooklink around the mainline when the rig is cast out. Although it's rare for the hooklength to spin as radically as some proponents of the rig imagine, it does slowly turn around the central hub like slow-moving helicopter rotor blades. This motion is essential in stopping the rig tangling, as the movement of the hooklink ensures it's stretched out on the cast and can't wrap itself around the line.

Furthermore the position of the leger on the end of the line produces an aerodynamic set-up that flies with minimum drag on the line. Many anglers use helicopter-style set-ups when they want to cast a long way.

On page 71 you'll see a development of the helicopter called the chod rig, but in this sequence we'll concentrate on how to tie two basic versions of the rig, one using a safe leadcore, the other using a pre-tied leader material.

The leadcore helicopter rig

1 Fox, E-S-P and Korda make ready-tied helicopter leadcore rigs to take the stress out of using leadcore. No splicing of the line is needed to create the loop at the top of the leader.

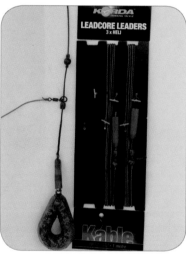

2 The leader is unravelled out of the pack.

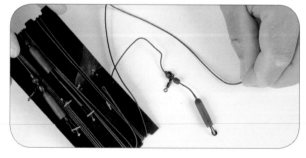

3 Then it's given a tug to straighten out the leadcore for better casting. It's very heavy and sinks like a stone, so it's unobtrusive.

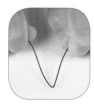

4 Attach your mainline to the leader using a grinner or Palomar knot.

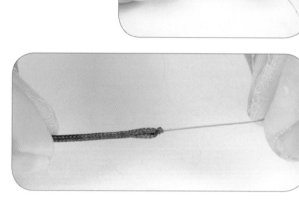

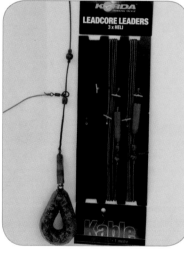

5 Clip on your lead.

6 Then slide the heli-bead down over the clip.

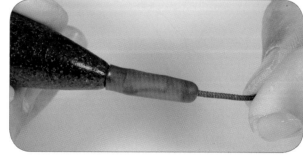

7 Adjust the sliding beads so that the rig will hang where you want it. The deeper the silt, or the thicker the weed, the further up the leader you might want to go.

8 Clip on your hooklength.

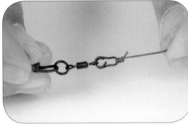

9 Cover the clip with a short length of silicone tubing.

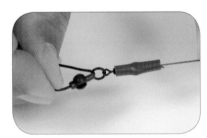

10 An alternative to silicone tubing is a cut-down anti-tangle sleeve, which can give a more streamlined result and help prevent tangles.

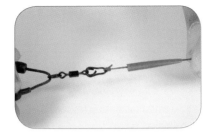

11 You're good to go, with a system that's great for distance fishing and keeps tangles to a minimum. When cast out, the hooklink rotates around the leadcore to stop tangles, and the leadcore pins itself to the lake bed.

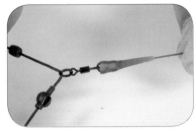

HOW THE HELICOPTER RIG WORKS

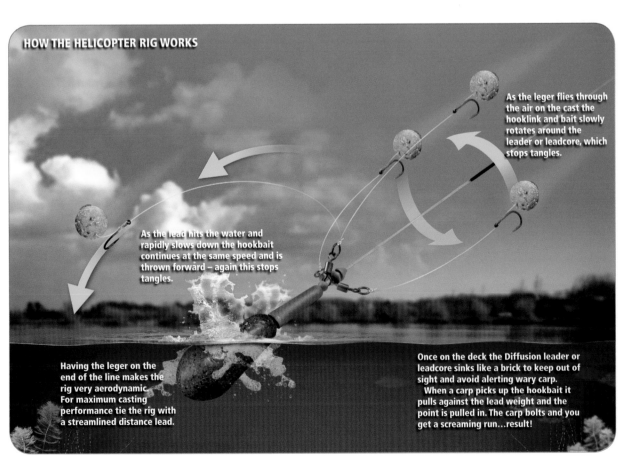

As the leger flies through the air on the cast the hooklink and bait slowly rotates around the leader or leadcore, which stops tangles.

As the lead hits the water and rapidly slows down the hookbait continues at the same speed and is thrown forward – again this stops tangles.

Having the leger on the end of the line makes the rig very aerodynamic. For maximum casting performance tie the rig with a streamlined distance lead.

Once on the deck the Diffusion leader or leadcore sinks like a brick to keep out of sight and avoid alerting wary carp.
When a carp picks up the hookbait it pulls against the lead weight and the point is pulled in. The carp bolts and you get a screaming run...result!

The pre-tied leader helicopter rig

1 This is a simple set-up that's used on waters where leadcore is banned. The Nash Helicopter leader has a set of beads and a swivel that rotates around a sinking leader.

2 Straighten out the Diffusion leader by giving it a pull, and tie the loop at the top to the mainline with a five-turn grinner knot.

3 Attach the leger to the clip on the bottom of the leader and use a Stik Klip or similar attachment to fix the hooklink to the leader. This is a coated braid link.

4 This carefully designed rig features beads and a wide-bore swivel that'll slide off the leader easily if the line snaps and the leger snags.

5 The bead stem gives protection to the leader line when a fish is hooked and the line is pulled at a 90° angle, which can snap the line if the swivel is placed directly on it.

Over the page you'll see how these rigs avoid tangles when they're cast out, and you'll also see how they lie on the lake bed.

The chod

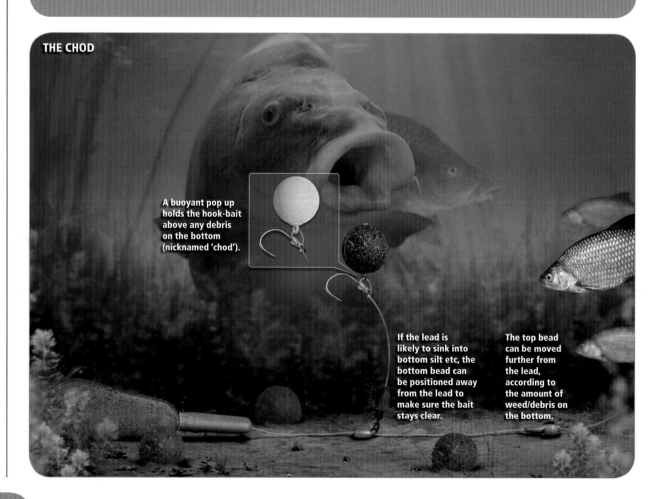

THE CHOD

A buoyant pop up holds the hook-bait above any debris on the bottom (nicknamed 'chod').

If the lead is likely to sink into bottom silt etc, the bottom bead can be positioned away from the lead to make sure the bait stays clear.

The top bead can be moved further from the lead, according to the amount of weed/debris on the bottom.

Tying up the chod rig

If there's a rig that's been written about more than the chod in recent years then I don't know what it is – this is the Spice Boy of the rig world!

In a nutshell, it's utterly simple in its construction and operation yet seems to have almost succumbed to folklore. Many anglers think it's almost invincible. Personally, I'm less of a chod fan than many other anglers, who've become followers of fashion, yet I can see it does work, and in weedy waters it delivers superb performance.

There are several companies selling ready-to-assemble chod systems, and I would thoroughly recommend them if you want to go down the chod rig route. Here I show you how to assemble one of the commercial kits and also the 'naked chod'. For the naked chod the rig itself isn't slipped on to leadcore or a leader, and I think it's far safer if a line breakage happens. Finally I also suggest a few chod tips that move it on.

The basic chod rig – assembling a chod kit

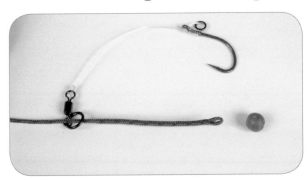

1 Unravel the leader and pull to straighten. Slide the components on to the leader.

2 Attach the lead via the lead clip.

3 Slide the rubber sleeve over the lead clip and push it till it meets the lead.

4 Adjust the beads to your personal preference.

How to tie up a naked chod rig

Basically the 'naked chod' is simply the same very short, stiff hooklength trapped between two beads. I like it (a) because I think it's far safer if a line breakage occurs, and (b) because I think it's a lot less obvious laying on the bottom.

1 You need a Korda Chod rig that looks as simple as it is to use!

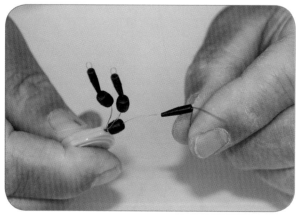

2 Thread the tungsten chod sleeve up the line...

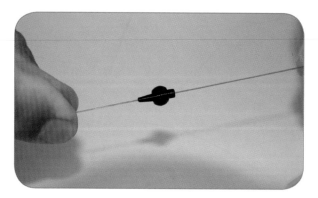

3 ...followed by the no-trace bead...

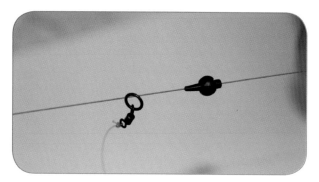

4 ...then a very short 3–5in hooklink.

5 Add the second barrel bead below the hooklink to trap it in place.

6 Slide on a helicopter lead rubber.

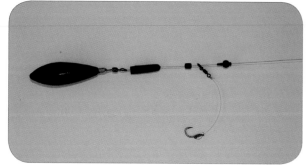

7 Tie on the leger (use a Palomar knot and make sure it's perfect, as all the playing of the fish relies on this one knot!) and cover the knot with a sleeve.

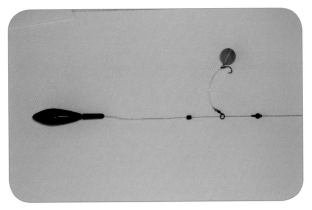

8 You now customise the position of the stops around the leger. (I slide the top bead around 2.5ft up the line with the bottom one 1ft above the lead.)

9 Tie a very buoyant pop-up on to the hooklink and counterbalance it with tungsten putty moulded round the top half of the swivel.

10 This is the finished rig – it's so simple to set up and use.

Chod rig tips and tweaks

You can give the rig a host of little tweaks that improve it in small but important ways. Here are two you might want to try…

Ace bait screws
This is a good tip for using pop-up boilies on almost any rig, not just the chod. It features a small peg screw that's wound into the bait until it bites tightly and doesn't budge.

I know some anglers lack confidence in this system, because a simple screw seems almost pathetic – surely the bait flies off on the cast, doesn't it? Well, no, it doesn't, and the system works a treat.

Make your own baits
Making pop-up boilies is a great way to make your own baits that don't soak up water and start to sink.

Get some boilie base mix and mix it up with eggs until it goes firm. Then mould it round a cork ball and seal the mixture round the ball.

Pop the ball into a pan of boiling water and cook for usually two minutes (but check the supplier's instructions). Take out and dry overnight on a towel.

The finished bait is permanently buoyant and won't sink – once it's tied on it stays popped-up.

The zig (anchored)

How to tie the zig rig

Despite being one of the most bizarre carping tactics, the zig is one of the best rigs to appear in recent years. In a nutshell it comprises a super-long hooklink baited with a very buoyant pop-up boilie that comes to rest stationed in the mid to upper layers of the water column.

Frankly it looks bizarre, and it does seem odd that carp just swim up to a bait sitting anchored in mid water and suck it in; yet they seem to lose much of the caution that makes them so difficult to catch on the bottom.

The following hooklink and hooking methods show how simple the rig is to set up and should give you plenty of ideas to boost your zig rigging. It's a very simple rig to set up, and the biggest challenge you'll probably have to overcome is the battle taking place in the grey matter between your ears. Catching on a super-long hooklink that's almost isolated in the middle of the water column requires you to adopt a wholly different mindset, but if you make the correct decisions on setting up you'll have added a brilliant rig to your armoury.

I'll also look at sloppy spodding in detail – a devastating little edge that can take some waters apart, especially during the summer and early autumn.

Tying up a basic zig rig

1 Tie a loop in buoyant line like Nash's Zig Line.

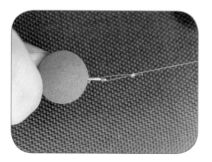

2 Attach a buoyant bait such as a pop-up boilie to the hair rig loop.

3 Use a knotless knot to attach the hook to the line.

4 Tie a size 8 swivel to the other end.

Try this for a change

An alternative choice of bait is the Nash Zig Bug. These bizarre creations mimic the size and shape of the floating insects that hit the water's surface, which the carp suck in and fill up on. They're a brilliant if somewhat bizarre creation that have caught fish from lots of waters.

Hair rig in exactly the same way as you do a normal hookbait and cast it out – the carp and the bait will do the rest.

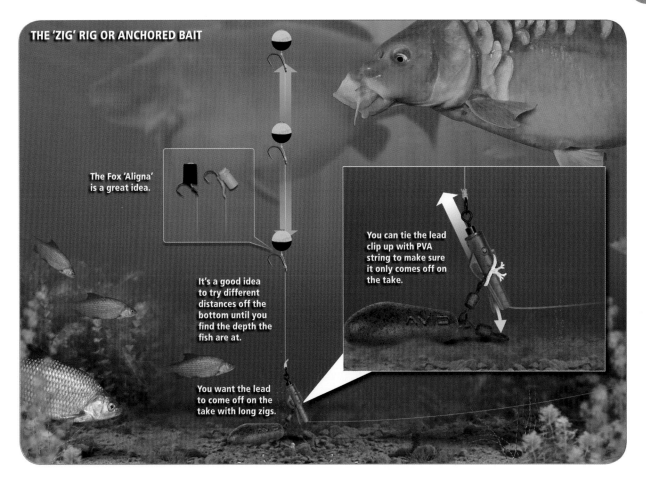

THE 'ZIG' RIG OR ANCHORED BAIT

The Fox 'Aligna' is a great idea.

It's a good idea to try different distances off the bottom until you find the depth the fish are at.

You want the lead to come off on the take with long zigs.

You can tie the lead clip up with PVA string to make sure it only comes off on the take.

This is a great idea

I also like this idea from Fox. Called the Aligna, it simplifies the whole notion of tying up a bait and works a treat.

At the centre of the rig are some small foam barrels in a variety of colours that have proved attractive to carp.

Also supplied with the rig are special fixings that go on the back of the hook, which hold the foam nugget in exactly the right position to hook a fish.

It makes the whole process of rigging up a zig rig far easier, and is a great advancement.

A couple of tips

Casting zigs and playing/netting fish hooked on long zigs can be tricky, so here are a couple of tips to help.

Firstly, I like to place my zig hookbait in a bucket when casting, so that it can't catch on anything as I cast.

Secondly, I dispense with the tail rubber on the lead clip and just tie the lead on with PVA string. The lead comes off as the fish takes, so I can play the fish direct.

CARP BAITS

Walk into any tackle shop these days and you need to beware that you don't get flattened by shelves collapsing under the weight of specialist carp baits! It's amazing to think that there was a time – not that long ago – when specialist carp bait meant a par boiled potato. These days, however, carp baits are as complicated as any human food, and you could easily get the feeling that men in white coats have been behind the creation of the many high-tech offerings available. Carp baits are now a science.

In this chapter we'll look first at the king of baits, the boilie. We'll look at what boilies are, what the differences are between them and how you make them. Following this we'll detail pellets, particle baits and finally natural offerings like maggots.

But before I delve into the sometime murky world of carp baits I want to issue a plea. Many anglers get utterly *obsessed* with baits, thinking that the lump of food they put on the end of their rig is far and away THE most important part of the fish-catching equation. It isn't. Modern baits are not an ultimate remedy to compensate for all your other mistakes or failings. There *is* no ultimate or irresistible bait, so don't get obsessed with what you put on the end of your

Boilies are balls of paste made with eggs and boiled until they go hard.

hooklink. It's simply the last piece of the carp-fishing jigsaw, and once you've got a few good offerings in your armoury you don't need to keep changing your bait as you search for something you won't find.

Anyway, lecture over. Let's look at carp baits!

What's a boilie?

Boilies are a collection of powdered ingredients that are bound together with eggs, made into a ball of paste, rolled into balls and then boiled to make them go hard. However, there's a huge range of different boilies, and they tend to attract fish in three ways: they either have a high nutritional value that the fish recognise; they're loaded with flavours and extracts that fish smell and are attracted by; or they combine both of these things to get the best of both sources of attraction.
Let's start by taking a brief look at the main types of boilie.

Many boilies contain a considerable quantity of fishmeal or crushed pellets. This not only gives the finished bait a

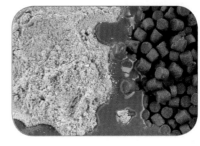

strong fishmeal smell and taste, but also boosts the nutritional value of the bait, as such baits are high in fish oil and protein.

Some baits build on this fishmeal content with the addition of fish extracts, oils and flavours – anchovy, squid, salmon and shrimp

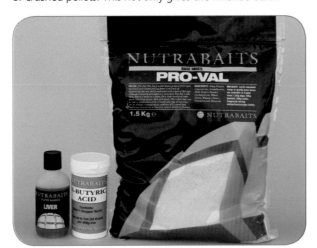

powder are commonly added to fishmeal baits to boost the fishy attraction of the finished bait.

Others have a base dominated by a high birdfood content and are made with lots of cereal and seeds. These boilies are

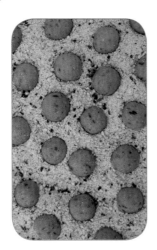

naturally attractive but they have a more neutral scent that can easily be boosted with flavours, colours and extracts to produce a finished bait that's both nutritious and highly attractive.

Yet other boilies have a more savoury appeal, with lots of powdered meat proteins and extracts like liver powder making up their content.

Finally, some boilies are made with an altogether blander base mixture made up of soya powder, semolina and milk proteins. Depending on the quantity of products used some baits are made mainly with lower nutritional value ingredients, such as soya powder. These baits are designed to be carriers for flavours and attractors that carp find appealing; these so-called attractor baits can prove very effective. At the other end of the scale are boilies with a much higher milk protein content, making them a far richer food source; these baits are sometimes called HNV (high nutritional value) boilies, and they attract fish that recognise the food signal they emit.

It's also important to realise that fishmeal, birdfood and savoury/meat protein baits contain milk protein and soya-style products to bulk them out, which also help them bind and aid the hardening process when the baits are cooked.

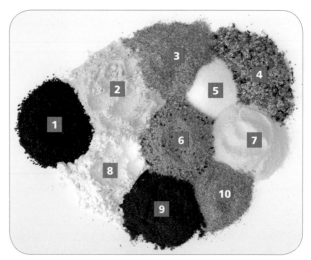

There's a wide range of potential ingredients:

1 Dried seaweed	5 Amino acid	8 Whey protein
2 Soya flour	6 Yellow bird food	9 Bird food
3 Wheat germ	7 Fine semolina	10 Wheat flour
4 Coarse birdfood		

DIFFERENT BOILIE TYPES

Cork ball pop-up – stays buoyant for a long time. Ideal on chods etc.

Adding coric dust to your basic base mix makes it buoyant enough to just stay off the bottom with the hook holding it down.

A standard pop-up can be trimmed to make it critically balanced.

Standard bottom bate fished on the bottom.

Shelf-life or freezer baits?

Whatever the ingredients of the boilie you choose, you'll then have to decide whether to buy fresh boilies that have been frozen, or boilies that have had a preservative added or undergone a special process in their manufacture to stop them going mouldy. Called 'shelf-life boilies', the latter are the ones you see lined up in tackle shops.

At one time this choice involved you making a simple decision. Shelf-life baits were relatively poor-quality boilies that were high on artificial flavour and low on nutritional value, whereas frozen boilies were better quality and highly nutritious. However, in recent years the quality of shelf-life baits has increased significantly, and freezer baits are no longer necessarily superior. Many bait firms have worked hard to produce better shelf-life baits, and it's now possible to buy perfectly good preserved baits that will consistently catch carp. Of course, there's also an obvious practical reason for choosing shelf-life baits – you don't need a freezer to store them!

However, it must be said that many great baits are indeed freshly frozen, and if you make your own boilies at home then you'll need to freeze them to stop them going mouldy.

Personally I use both shelf-life and freezer boilies. As a rule I use high-attract shelf-life boilies when I'm fishing relatively heavily stocked waters, or when I'm fishing in the depths of winter and want a supremely attractive bait that's loaded with colour and flavour to grab a fish's attention.

By contrast, when I'm fishing waters that have a lower

Nutrabaits Trigga Ice, one of my all-time favourites.

stock of fish and often bigger carp that have seen it all before I prefer to use what I perceive to be higher quality frozen boilies that are attractive but also very nutritious. These baits tend to be more expensive, but in my opinion you often get a better bait for your money.

Whether you pick shelf-life or frozen baits always make sure you buy baits made by a reputable company. The bulk of the baits I've used for the last 25 years have been made by Nutrabaits, and I have the utmost confidence in the products they produce. Their Trigga Ice frozen boilie is my favourite bait of all time and is the one I use for 90% of my fishing – it'll take something truly staggering to make me change!

That said, I have used baits from other firms, like Solar, Nash, Dynamite, Richworth and Mainline, and many of my friends have a similar level of faith in the baits they get from these firms as I have in Nutrabaits.

So the motto of the story is this. By all means try different baits and experiment as you find your feet in the world of carp fishing. But once you've found a couple of different baits that you're confident in, then stick with them, and don't change just because of one bad trip – good baits don't become bad ones overnight.

Nutrabaits owner Bill Cottam, my long-time friend and advisor on 'matters boilie'.

A well-stocked bait freezer.

What size to go for?

A range of sizes can be an advantage. So too can alternative shapes, such as barrel, for more wary fish.

Most good baits are available in a range of sizes and even shapes. The most popular sizes are between 14mm and 20mm diameter, and it probably makes relatively little difference which size you pick. However, there are a few issues to consider before you pick a bait size, as in certain circumstances it might make a difference.

Most obviously the distance you're fishing and want to feed your bait at does affect the size of boilie you pick. If you're fishing at 80 yards you'll not be able to catapult your bait that far unless you're using a round and relatively big boilie of 18mm or 20mm. A lightweight 12mm bait simply won't fly that far.

On some waters where large numbers of bream and tench are present a big bait of at least 18mm will be needed in order to avoid catching a succession of fish you don't want to catch! Of course, you might not mind catching bream and tench while you wait for a carp, in which case a 12mm bait will get you lots of action.

Personally I prefer to use smaller baits where I can. A dinky 12mm boilie is a more natural size of food item for a carp to eat, as it's similar to the size of snails and the like which make up a large part of its natural diet. A carp feeding on a spread of 12mm baits also has to pick up more boilies than it would if it was eating gobstoppers of 20mm. This increases how long the carp stays in your baited area, and therefore increases the chance of it sucking in your hookbait.

Using small baits like this means I can use smaller, lighter hooks that are less obtrusive, and on waters where everyone is using 18mm or 20mm baits using mini boilies can give you an element of surprise that can be a major edge.

Indeed, doing something different with your bait is why different-shaped baits can work well. Several bait firms produce barrel-shaped boilies that look different to standard-issue round ones and many anglers use scissors or gadgets like the Korda Kutter to turn round boilies into halved or haphazardly shaped baits.

For longer range you might need larger baits.

Personally I like smaller baits.

And don't forget your pop-ups

Finally, no matter what type of boilie you choose don't forget that you'll also need to carry buoyant pop-up boilies for use as a specialist hookbait. As you'll see in this chapter and in the previous one, there are many rig set-ups that make use of baits that pop up off the lake bed. In some cases this simply produces a different set-up that can trip up a curious fish, but in many cases a pop-up bait is used to ensure thick weed, silt or debris doesn't mask the bait from a carp.

My kit always includes a range of pop-up baits that can be called on when I need them. I usually carry some cork-balled Trigga Ice pop-ups that match the free offerings I use, but there are many other really good ones to choose from, some coming ready flavoured, some with pots of additional flavour to dip the pop-up into. I really rate the Solar and Nash ranges. I often use these bright and very smelly baits over a bed of dark brown Trigga Ice boilies and they catch a lot of carp. In my mind this odd-one-out acts like a target bait for a carp to aim at when entering the baited area. It's amazing how often the one bright popped-up 'target bait' I've cast out is taken first.

Pop-ups can be a valuable addition to your hookbait options.

Two of my favourites from the Nash and Solar ranges.

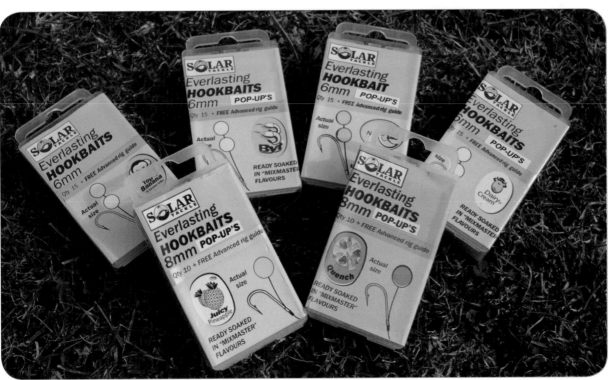

Boilie-making at home

While many anglers buy frozen or shelf-life baits, a good number of carpers still prefer to make their own, a process that allows them to customise their bait to a certain recipe that may well give them a fishing edge, especially on heavily fished venues where the fish have had just about every bait ever made thrown at them for years. Knowing how a boilie is made is also a good way to improve your overall understanding of what carp like to eat.

First I'll look at how a standard boilie is made, then I'll look at an easy way to make some pop-ups to go with them.

1 The equipment you need: a bowl, scales, fork, whisk, spoon, boilie rolling system, sieve, pan and a drying tray with a cloth.

2 As for the bait ingredients you'll need a boilie base mix (the powdered ingredients that make up the bait), eggs and any flavours or additives you want to put in the bait.

3 All good bait firms include mixing instructions with their boilie base mix. Don't ignore these directions, as every mix will behave slightly differently.

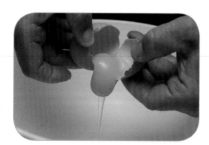

4 Crack the eggs into a bowl. In most cases the recipes suggested will be for a four-egg or six-egg mix.

5 Add the liquid additives to the eggs. These products have suggested dosages, and it's important not to exceed them. More flavour doesn't mean more fish, so have a range of measuring spoons handy.

6 I prefer adding natural extracts to my baits, as I believe the natural food signal the bait then has is highly attractive to carp.

7 However, I do add a small dose of artificial flavour to boost the attraction offered by the final bait.

8 Mix the ingredients thoroughly.

9 You can at this stage add a colour if you wish. Most of the powdered colours are very concentrated, so you need very little to colour your bait. Sprinkle a small amount on and mix again.

10 Now you add the base mix powder. Mix the measured powder to the eggs a bit at a time. Be aware that the suggested quantity of base mix is only a guide, so don't add too much to start with.

11 Fork it in.

12 Keep adding and mixing until it starts to stiffen, then start kneading it into a smooth paste.

13 You're looking to create a soft, smooth paste that doesn't stick to your hands when you mould it – this indicates it will roll well.

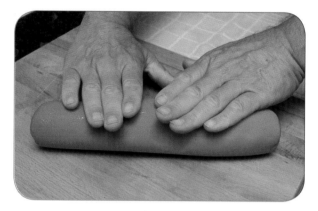

14 Roll out into a large sausage.

15 Cut into smaller chunks.

16 Roll out into thin sausages using the rolling guide that's part of your rolling-table system.

17 Note: if, long-term, you're going to make lots of boilies on a regular basis, it's well worth investing in a metal bait gun with a range of nozzles, which will make producing the sausages very quick and easy.

18 Place a sausage of soft boilie paste on the rolling table; the sausage should match the width of the table. Try to be quite quick in order to stop the paste drying out, which might hinder rolling. Push down the top half of the table to cut the sausage.

19 Run the top half of the table back and forth, trapping barrels of soft paste between the two halves of the table. This produces perfectly round balls of paste that are now ready for boiling to make the bait go hard.

20 Repeat until all your paste is rolled.

21 Different base mixes usually suggest different cooking times – most often between one and two minutes to produce a firm bait. As a rough rule of thumb, most boilies float as their cooking time nears its end. Don't add too many baits to the pan at once. Also, agitate the sieve from time to time to make sure they cook evenly and don't stick to each other.

22 When they're cooked, lift them out of the water in the sieve, drain them, and lay them on a towel to dry, cool and harden. Leave the baits for at least a few hours, or better still overnight to fully dry off – bagging up too soon traps lots of condensation in the bag.

23 Bag up and place in the freezer. Get a cheap chest freezer to store your baits in rather than using the family food freezer – fishmeal-tainted pizzas aren't nice!

Consider a rolling service

In all truth, rolling boilies is a time-consuming bore, and if you have a busy family or work life, spending hours making bait may not be a realistic option. Obviously, this is why so many ready-made shelf-life and frozen boilies are sold through tackle shops, but you can also employ the services of a specialist bait-rolling company to supply fresh freezer bait to your own specification.

After making my own baits for many years I started using one of these companies because I was finding I didn't have time to make my boilies. I have to say that having done this I'll probably never make another boilie again! Yes, it's obviously a bit more expensive than doing it yourself, but in my opinion it takes away so much hassle that it really is worth it.

The company I use is called Rollin Baits (www.rollinbaits. net), but there are several others that produce high-quality bait on time. A visit to Rollin's factory gives you an insight into how boilies are made to your specifications in large quantities.

The dry ingredients are carefully measured into the mixer.

Mixing is carefully timed and monitored.

The end product is cut and checked for consistency.

The paste is rolled into large sausages for the pressure gun.

Long thin sausages of paste come out of the gun on to the rolling table.

After cutting and rolling they're checked for roundness etc...

...then brushed into a holding tray.

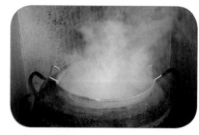
Boil time will depend on required hardness.

The boilies are lifted out on to drying trays where they're spread out to dry out thoroughly.

Rollin will roll to your own specifications using bait from any of the major bait companies, but it does have close links to Nutrabaits.

Rollin produce almost all my frozen boilies and do the same for my friend Brian Skoyles, here seen picking up our bait for a French trip.

If you want to go for the frozen bait option but prefer to leave its design to 'bait experts' then several companies supply excellent ranges of frozen bait direct to tackle shops, the Nash Monster Squid being one of the most popular.

Boilie making on an industrial scale.

Flavours and colours go into the eggs.

Thoroughly mixed.

The base mix is added.

The mix before and after.

The finished mix goes into the extruder.

Boilie sausages are extruded and cut to size.

Sausages drop into the rollers.

Rolled boilies are regularly checked for quality.

Rolled baits enter the cauldron.

Finished baits coming off the production line.

Cooled and air-dried.

Bagged up.

Making pop-ups

Once you've made your bottom baits it's a good idea to make some pop-ups to match them at the same time.

'Cork-balling' is a quick and easy way to make a few pop-ups that perfectly match your bottom baits. Here's a quick guide to making pop-up boilies with a cork ball in the centre of them so that they mimic the free offerings.

Cork ball pop-ups

1 When you're making your main boilies, save a small quantity of the paste.

2 Pull off a small chunk, flatten it, and place a cork ball in the middle.

3 Roll the paste around the cork ball, ensuring you use enough paste to wrap the cork ball in several millimetres of bait. Boil as before, although you'll need to experiment with the cooking time – it usually takes less time to produce a hard skin around the cork ball.

4 Allow the baits to dry and harden as before, then bag up and freeze.

Consider drizzling a bit of attractor on the baits when you lift them out of the freezer. This bait booster is drawn into the outer layer to boost the source of smell.

High-attract pop-ups

Several bait companies sell tubs of pop-ups, and there's a huge range of colours and flavours. These can be made even more 'high-attract' by using a flavour spray or a booster liquid.

Boosting your hookbaits

Having dealt with how to make freezer boilies and produce pop-ups, you now know the basics of how to make bait that will catch you a lot of fish. Next I'm going to deal with the subject of attractors and the thorny subject of what flavours and extracts you can add to your boilie mix when you make bait – in other words, how to customise your bait to a specific recipe.

Don't overload your bait

The first thing to realise is that, as I've already said, more flavour does *not* mean more fish. Just loading a bait with more and more flavour and colour means that it eventually reaches a point where the smell and taste become so strong that they repel fish rather than attract them.

Carp are acutely aware of their surroundings and have a sense of smell and taste that's far more finely tuned than ours. Consequently they can pick up flavours that would be far too weak for us to register. I've never forgotten this fact.

In my carp fishing I've graduated towards using free offerings that have a muted source of attraction, and I mainly rely on natural food signals to attract carp. Instead of making baits that stink to high heaven I produce baits with a natural smell that isn't too potent – I know the carp can smell it.

Overload your hookbaits

Now comes the slightly contradictory bit! After having just advised you not to overload your boilies with flavour, and singing the praises of using natural attractors that give your bait a more muted source of attraction, here comes the point where I rip all this up and advocate using hookbaits that stink!

For many years I've used what I term 'target baits', where the hookbait is soaked (or glugged) in liquid attractors to produce a hookbait with added kick. Used on its own amid free offerings that haven't been loaded with extra flavour, the hookbait becomes the focal point for a carp's feeding activity. I've watched carp home-in on the glugged bait and pick it up first, leaving all the free offerings behind.

The key thing to realise is that you're boosting one bait, not dozens of freebies, so the source of attraction isn't too high. Furthermore, there are times when having a hookbait that screams out a potent smell signal can make the difference between a blank session and a bite.

Winter is a time when carp can be difficult to tempt and can be reluctant feeders, but at this time of year the fish can be coaxed into sucking up a smelly target bait compared to a more normal boilie with a muted smell.

Now that I've given you some idea how attractors should be utilised let's look at some products that could be used.

Concentrated flavours

These liquid additives are the simplest form of attractor that can be added to a bait. Although there are slight differences between various types of flavour, in a nutshell these attractors are highly concentrated liquids that use chemicals to produce a substance that mimics the smell and taste of food items. There are literally hundreds of different flavours available, and as I'm repeatedly asked to recommend individual products here are my favourites.

Nutrabaits and Mainline Pineapple

I often have 2–3ml of pineapple flavour added to each pound of base mix that's to be made into boilies. This provides a background smell to the finished bait. It's also a good flavour when used in combination with another unusual attractor, Nutrabaits N-Butyric Acid. Although it's an exotic-sounding liquid, this potent substance is a natural extract from animal fats. It's an extremely pungent attractor that's strangely  attractive to fish. Use just a drop or two per pound of bait, and don't spill it anywhere – you'll never remove the stink!

Nutrabaits and Richworth Tutti Frutti

A classic fish catcher that's been around for years but which still catches an awful lot of carp. Use 4–5ml per pound of boilie base mix.

Nash Scopex

One of the all-time top carp catchers, and while it's been on the scene for over 20 years it shows no sign of running out of steam. Use 4–5ml per pound of bait.

Solar Squid and Octopus

This is a more complicated and expensive type of flavour, but what a cracker it is. In fishmeal baits this takes some beating when 2-10ml is added to each pound of base mix.

Nutrabaits Blue Oyster

This is a new flavour that I've been using for a year at the time of writing, but it has the sort of instant fish-catching performance that can't be ignored. Used at around 10ml per pound of base mix this lovely smell isn't a really potent fishy flavour; it's a more subtle, rounded flavour, but one that many carp find instantly attractive.

Natural extracts

These substances are made out of natural products and are loaded with proteins and amino acids that scream out a natural food signal to a carp.

I always fish with boilies that have been enhanced with extracts, and listed below are my favourites. I often soak or glug my baits in these natural flavours to give them a boost. Setting them apart from concentrated flavours, you can use far more of these natural products, with 10–30ml per pound being generally advised.

Nutrabaits Nutramino

The ingredients list on the bottle sounds like a horror film – this treacle-like liquid contains gastric mucosa, liver and fresh spleen. Originally made as a liquid food to be given to seriously ill patients struggling to digest solid food, similar substances are produced by many bait firms, and all catch carp by the thousand.

Loaded with protein, this potent liquid not only boosts the smell and taste of your bait but also boosts the 'food' signal it leaks. Use 20ml per pound of bait.

Dynamite Source liquid

Another classic additive that proves every year just how good it is. Not dissimilar to Nutramino, Source liquid is loaded with natural substances like liver, but there's also a background smell that carp love. Use 3–5ml per egg. Like all these extracts it can be drizzled on rolled baits to boost their attraction.

Nash Sweetcorn extract

This is a very unusual product, which unlike most of the other extracts listed here isn't loaded with natural proteins. Instead, this gloopy liquid is loaded with natural sugars and has a sweet smell that carp adore.

I really rate corn extract, but I use it slightly differently to other extracts. Instead of adding it to my bait at the mixing stage I store my plastic baits in the stuff, and also dip a hookbait boilie in it. I never go fishing without a glug pot loaded with fake baits stored in corn extract. I should also

mention that the person who tipped me off about it was actually sponsored by a rival bait company – that proves how good it is!

Nutrabaits Green Lipped Mussel powder
This fine powder is loaded with betaine and other proven fish attractors. I've used it for years, and it shows no sign of losing its appeal to carp.

Nash Shellfish and Regular Amino Liver Sense Appeal
Sense Appeals create irresistible water born smells or food signals so they attract carp to the bait. They can also induce heavy and competitive feeding which can improve the chances of a fish making a mistake with the hook bait. The Amino profile provides carp with a beneficial food source. Added to a base mix they significantly boost the food value of the finished bait. They can be used on their own but are particularly effective when combined with flavours and Oil Palatants. Although anglers tend to class them as natural attractors they are actually 'tweaked' slightly in the Nash Bait lab and are part natural, part synthetic.

Amino Liver can be used at relatively high levels – recommended levels for a 4 egg mix are up to 20ml although some anglers have done very well at higher levels, particularly in winter. It can also be used neat as a bait dip.

Inclusion rates for Shellfish Concentrate are up to 7ml in a 4 egg mix. Again it's an additive that combines well with other attractors, eg Shellfish and Scopex mixed 50/50 is a very effective combination and rated by Gary Bayes as one of the very best attractor combinations for use in spring.

Natural oils

These liquids produce a similar level of food signal to liquid liver products like Nutramino. Loaded with fish proteins, they're highly attractive to carp, and they make a great additive to almost every fishmeal or crushed pellet-based boilie. Although they will catch fish in winter these baits work best in the warmer months of the year, when the oil leaches into the water more efficiently.

Once again they can be used at levels of between 10 and 30ml per pound of bait. They can also be drizzled on baits before they thaw, and baits can be stored in the oil. I've caught lots of carp on fishmeal boilies that are glugged in 50ml of salmon oil laced with 5ml of Nutrabaits Tutti Frutti flavour.

Sweeteners

The finishing touch for many baits is the addition of a sweetener. Not only do carp like sweet things, but these liquids tone down the flavours in the bait and produce a more palatable final offering.

Just as you have to stick to the recommended dosage levels stated on the labels of flavourings, so you also have to limit the amount of sweetener you use.

Nutrabaits Sweet Cajouser is my favourite sweetener, and 2ml per pound of finished bait is a great addition to any finished boilie. Hinders Betalin is also a great additive that I've used with considerable success.

Bringing it all together

The best baits carry a range of additives and attractors that complement each other well. A toned-down amount of flavour (2–3ml) blended with 20–30ml of extract and 1–2ml of sweetener will produce an attractive bait that's neither too strong-smelling nor too weak to be effective. This is the perfect bait to be a long-term carp catcher.

Ten great boilie tips

Here are ten ideas to boost your boilie fishing. As I've said before, bait isn't the magic bullet that catches carp no matter how you fish, but having faith in your bait allows you to forget about it and concentrate on getting the other bits of the equation right.

It might sound a bit daft, but I firmly believe that having a bait in which you have total faith means you can spend more time concentrating on where the fish are and how they're feeding.

1 The plastic snowman

I'm a huge fan of this simple set-up. It uses a 12mm Nutrabaits Trigga Ice freezer boilie flavoured with Blue Oyster, that's then capped off with a piece of Enterprise Tackle's plastic corn that's been soaked in Nash Sweetcorn extract. Looks odd, but catches carp.

2 Bits and pieces

On waters where large, round boilies are used by everyone, trimming the edges off the bait to change their round profile can give you an edge. Glugging the bait in fish oil or natural extracts is an extra advantage, as removing the skin off the bait makes it more porous. As a bonus, use the bits in a small PVA mesh bag

3 Be bright

Carry a range of fluoro-coloured pop-up boilies and use them on their own or as a 'snowman' set-up with a sinking bait. I rate Solar's range of pop-up baits, which are supplied in a screw-lid pot with a small 'Pot Shot' tub of liquid additive. This allows the bait to be regularly boosted as it dries out.

4 Crush them

Boilies are attractive, but crushed boilies are super-attractive. Loaded into a PVA mesh bag and attached to the hook, these baits focus attention on the hookbait.

5 Go small

Many anglers routinely use large boilies with an 18mm diameter, and carp can get used to the large profile of these baits. Each bait also provides the fish with a sizeable snack. Cutting bait size down to 10 or 12mm not only produces a bait that looks different and is therefore less suspicious but it also rewards the fish with a smaller quantity of food for each bait they eat. This means they must feed longer and pick up more baits to achieve the same level of sustenance. The more baits they pick up, the more likely it is that they'll pick up the one attached to the hook.

6 Go large!

For the very opposite reasons to those stated above, huge 20 or 22mm baits can give you an edge where everyone else is using standard 14mm baits straight out of the bag.

7 Slow sinker

Using a bait that's been drilled out and plugged with cork, or produced by mixing a pop-up mix with a boilie base mix, creates a finished bait that has almost neutral buoyancy, so

the bait just drops to the bottom. Negating the weight of the hook in this way makes the finished rig more likely to trip up wary fish that can spot 'heavy' baits.

8 Shot on the hook

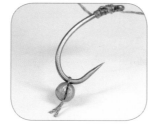

Pinning down a buoyant pop-up boilie with a split shot pinched to a piece of braid wrapped round the bend of a hook produces a bait that sits up at an angle on the lake bed and is easily sucked up by a carp. However, most significantly of all the shot weighs down the hook to drop the point into the lower lip – the perfect hook-hold position.

9 Long-term glugs

Some of my glug pots have had baits in them for nearly ten years, and I think they're getting better with age! The glug liquid dries out slightly to form a treacly gunk that sticks to the baits like glue and really boosts the bait. From late autumn to early spring I carry a pot of Nutrabaits Tecni-spice boilies soaked in 50ml of their Bait Soak Complex laced with

5ml of Sweet Nutraspice flavouring. This spicy bait is one I rate in cold water, and these baits honestly get better by the year. My friend Brian Skoyles turned me on to this bait a decade ago, and the pots I laced up then are still being used today.

Once you've got a winning recipe, fill two or three pots with bait, glug them in flavour and leave them to mature like finest Scotch whisky!

10 Paste wrap

This is another way to boost your hookbait, but allows you to do it with a boilie paste that's identical to the free offerings in every way apart from the fact that it hasn't been boiled. With no skin on the bait it leaks flavours far better, and produces a more attractive final offering that can also be dappled with seeds or tiny pellets to add to the source of attraction.

PARTICLES

If boilies have become the top bait of the modern carp scene, particle baits are the second string, used as feed baits and – in the case of the larger particles – the hookbait too. In this chapter I'll describe the six different groups of particle bait – seeds, beans, peas, nuts, pellets and naturals – and give details of the best ways to prepare and use them for feeding or on the rig itself.

Seeds

Companies such as Hinders provide a whole range of quality particles.

As you might expect, seed baits are just about the smallest type of carp bait, and in all but the most extreme circumstances they're only used as feed baits.

The advantage seeds have over other baits is their size. They're so tiny that they closely replicate the natural food items the carp feed on in any fishery. They also keep fish feeding for a long period of time, as they must graze on a carpet of feed in order to satisfy their hunger.

There are literally dozens of different seeds you could use, but I honestly think you only really need to look at hemp, Partiblend and maize.

Partiblend

This blend of seeds is actually the creation of particle bait specialists Hinders, although a few other suppliers have launched their own versions in recent years.

The idea is to create a bait that offers a whole host of different flavours and attractors that leak out of the individual seeds. In this mix you'll find red dari, white dari, hemp, groats, millet and linseed, tares and buckwheat, amid a mass of tiny offerings, and each seed has its own taste and smell that carp find attractive.

Prepare it in the same way as hemp – soak overnight, bring to the boil and simmer for 20–25 minutes. This makes

the seeds swell up and soften, while the cooking process activates the individual attractors that are bound up inside the seed. This turns the cooking water into a highly attractive soup that sticks to the seeds and leaks into the water.

Hemp

Arguably the ultimate individual seed bait, as these tiny black baits are loaded with natural oils and nutty flavours that carp find inherently attractive. The hard, crunchy shell of the seed also replicates the texture of natural food items like water snails and mussels, and it seems like carp might actually like crunching on things.

The sound of fish cracking open the seeds will be heard by other carp, and underwater filming suggests that this is actually a key attractor. As fish lay into the seeds they make a lot of disturbance that alerts others, which then come to investigate what's going on. This gives rise to a golden rule: feeding carp are the best attractor for other carp.

Carp of all sizes like hemp and there's no need to add flavours to make the seeds more attractive – they're loaded with so many natural attractors that they simply can't be added to. Soak in water overnight, bring to the boil then simmer for 20–30 minutes until the shell splits open and the white kernel is exposed. This allows the flavour to flood out.

COOKING HEMP

Put your dry hemp in an old pan.

Cover with water and leave overnight.

Bring to the boil and simmer for 25 minutes.

Check to see that the majority of the seeds have split.

Pour into your bait bucket, keeping the same liquid.

Perfectly cooked hemp 'ready to go'. Great tip: use the liquid to mix with groundbait or to soak boilies in!

LEFT: Maize, a proven top catcher of carp all over the world.

BELOW: Maize is easy to prepare and tougher than sweetcorn.

Maize

This is a real favourite of mine, and I can't understand why it's drifted into the shadows so much in recent years – it's an all-time carp catching classic.

Note I've picked maize, not sweetcorn. Maize is a much larger and tougher bait than corn, so it's more selective, more resistant to small fish activity, and can be cast for miles. Corn is a great bait, but in many waters maize has the edge.

A great tactic is to combine a piece of real maize with a piece of artificial pop-up maize, to create a balanced wafter/combo.

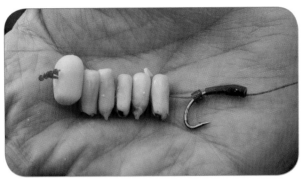

For a bigger bait, try a string of maize topped off with plastic.

Sweetcorn is a brilliant bait that carp love, but not quite as tough as maize.

I soak maize for 24 hours then slowly cook it until the grains start to split open, releasing a milky liquid that carp love. A great bait, and very underrated.

French Mix

Just before I leave seeds, just a few words about another of my favourites. I was originally shown this particles combination by my good friend Brian Skoyles. It's a combination of Partiblend, groats and flaked maize, the idea being that it combines the holding power of Partiblend, the visible attraction of the flaked maize and the flavour-carrying potential of the groats. Originally it was mixed for the large waters in France, hence the nickname 'French Mix', but

take my word for it, it's a great particle combination anywhere. The picture sequence shows how to flavour and prepare it. You can mix the blend yourself or get it ready-mixed from Hinders.

PREPARING FRENCH MIX

Two-thirds fill a bucket with dry mix and add a tin of evaporated milk.

Add any extra liquid flavour attractors (I use Nutrabaits Multimino).

Fill the bucket with water.

Stir thoroughly.

Leave for 24 hours – in the sun is fine, as it helps the swelling process. In winter you might need to transfer to a pan and just bring it to the boil.

Ready to go. Carp love it, and it has the potential to attract and hold the fish in the swim for long periods of time.

Beans and peas

Beans and peas – there are plenty to choose from, and some are great carp catchers.

I've lumped these two families of particle together because they're so similar, not only in size but also in the way they're prepared. Once again there are lots of different types of bait available, but I'll make it easier for you to cut through the massive choice by focusing in on a few well-proven offerings.

Black-eyed beans

This is one of the original particle baits, and although they've become less popular in recent years they're still good fish catchers, probably due to their bright and contrasting colour palette and slightly nutty taste.

Soak overnight to soften the bean and make it swell up. Cook for 10–20 minutes until the bean has become soft enough to slide on to a baiting needle but is still firm enough so that it doesn't disintegrate when it goes on the hair rig.

Like most beans it can easily be flavoured, as the bait

swells up so much that it soaks up additives like a sponge. Once in the water it then leaks this flavouring to attract carp. Add 5ml of Scopex flavour and 2ml of Sweet Cajouser to each pound of cooked beans and leave to soak for a few hours. As an even easier option, just buy a tin!

Maple peas

These little round, mottled peas are one of the all-time classic particle baits. Not only do carp like them, but their robust texture means they're excellent hair rig baits. Also, because they're so round and fairly heavy they catapult accurately and land in a neat spread.

Soak in water overnight, bring them to the boil then

simmer for 10–20 minutes. Like all natural particles cooking them is a slightly vague process, as different batches cook at different speeds. Keep checking the baits as they cook and remove them from the heat and drain off the cooking water before the skin splits and they go mushy.

They don't need to be flavoured, but adding 2ml of Sweet Cajouser or Betalin per pound of peas does produce a slightly tastier bait.

Chick peas

This bait is a real favourite of mine – when I was learning to carp fish on a very tight budget I used a lot of 'chicks', and caught countless fish on them.

While carp do like plain, cooked peas, what I really like about this bait is just how well it takes colour and flavour. My favourite recipe is to soak the hard peas overnight, bring them to the boil and then simmer for 15–20 minutes. As with all particles, keep an eye on the bait as they boil, and keep testing peas to check when they've softened. That way you can then remove them from the heat before they overcook and become mushy.

Drain off the cooking water, and while the peas are still warm (ie while the pores of the bait are still open) add 5ml of Nash Scopex flavour and 2ml of Sweet Cajouser to each pound of cooked bait. Leave overnight and in the morning you've got a hugely attractive bait that hair rigs and catapults well. It's a super-cheap bait too.

Nuts

Nuts come in all shapes and sizes. Most will catch carp, but I'm going to concentrate on two of the all-time greatest carp baits: tiger nuts and peanuts. Although their use has been controversial at times, when used responsibly they're a tremendous string to your bow – and make no mistake about it, carp *love* eating them. But before I deal with how to get the best from these baits, I'll deal first with the controversy.

Nuts have been banned on many waters because they've been blamed for poisoning carp and causing them physical damage when they swell up inside the fish. The truth is that a properly prepared food-grade nut that isn't thrown into the lake in huge quantities is no threat to carp. All nuts should be soaked for 24 hours, brought to the boil, then thoroughly cooked so that they swell fully and soften slightly. They're superb hookbaits and are best used with just a handful of free offerings.

Tiger nuts

Preservative-free tiger nuts are loaded with natural sugars that carp find very attractive. When they're bought the nut is rock hard and shrivelled up. Soaking starts the swelling process and then cooking does the rest. A half-hour cook is the *minimum* requirement, but bigger nuts may need at least 45 minutes in the pan.

They can then be used straight away, but I prefer to let the tigers ferment for a few days, which allows the sugars in the cooking water to turn into a gloopy syrup that carp adore. When I've cooked the nuts (often called 'growlers') I put them in a bucket, snap the lid on, and then leave them standing in the sun or somewhere warm for at least two or three days. This way the nuts turn horribly sticky but are much better than the freshly cooked baits.

COOKING TIGERS

Put your dry tigers in an old pan.

Cover with water and leave overnight.

Check that they've fully swollen.

Bring to the boil and cook for 45 minutes.

Once cooked they can be used straight away...

...but I prefer to put them in a bait bucket for two to three days till the liquid becomes 'gloopy'. Lovely!

Peanuts

These were one of the first baits I ever caught a carp on, and I still like to use them. Unlike tiger nuts, which can't really be overcooked, the trick with peanuts is cooking them long enough so that they swell fully but not so long that the thin skin wrapped round the bait splits open and the nut separates into its two halves.

Different batches of nut cook in different times, but as a rule you should soak them for 24 hours, bring to the boil, then simmer for 20–30 minutes. Test the nuts as they cook and you'll soon learn to tell when they're well prepared.

Like tigers, one or two peanuts should be threaded on a hair rig and just a handful or two scattered around the area with a spod or catapult.

A general guide to particle preparation

Throughout this chapter I've given guidance on soaking/cooking various particles and provided picture sequences for some of them. But it's important to get this right for all particles, so please use the following as a preparation checklist:

■ Put the baits in a pan and cover with water. If you're cooking baits that will swell up a lot – like hemp, tiger nuts and chick peas – make sure the baits are covered by several inches of water, so that the baits remain underwater all the time they're boiling.

■ Bring the baits to the boil. With the lid on the pan, turn down to simmer. Beans and peas take the least cooking – 10–20 minutes – while nuts take up to 45 minutes to swell. These natural baits vary slightly in how long it takes for them to swell up.

■ Baits like hemp should split, but chick peas and peanuts become useless if they halve. Always keep an eye on the bait during the cooking process to stop it overcooking. Beans and peas should then be drained to stop them going mushy, while nuts and seeds should remain in the cooking water while they cool.

Pellets

There's a huge range of pellets to pick from.

This is a modern family of particle baits that in recent years has become more popular than traditional seeds, beans, peas and nuts.

Produced by compressing and extruding fishmeal, oil and bulking agents, the pellets are cooked until they go hard. Cylindrical in shape, they start to soften as soon as they hit the water and then break down into a fine mush, releasing attractors as they do so.

There are dozens of different types of pellet on the market and it's no secret that 'different' baits from rival companies are in fact exactly the same pellet that's been bought in from one of the big processing companies and re-bagged. Yep, exactly the same bait will be for sale in the same shop from different companies!

I'll list my favourite pellets, but it's certainly not an exhaustive list and there are many others that will do just as good a job.

Halibut pellets

These are oily baits that break down fairly slowly and in doing so give off a slick of flavour that carp find very attractive. Pellets of 3–6mm are ideal to be spodded (see Chapter 9) and used as a mass feed bait, while larger 14–16mm pellets are drilled out and loaded on to the hair rig and used as hookbaits.

Salmon fry crumb/micro pellets/ Little Gemz

These tiny pellets are ideal for spodding or packing into solid PVA bags. Their microscopic size means the gaps between individual baits is minimised and the final PVA parcel can

become very tight indeed. This means the final bag can be made very aerodynamic and cast a long, long way.

Nutrabaits Trigga Ice pellets

Lots of bait firms produce pellets that have been boosted with extra attractors, and by all means use whichever of them you feel most confident with. Personally I love using Trigga Ice frozen boilies, so using pellets that are loaded with similar attractors and releasing them quickly as they break down is a great combination.

Dynamite Baits Source pellets

I mentioned in Chapter 6 that a boilie made using Source liquid is a true classic and will catch carp for evermore, and, unsurprisingly,

Source pellets are also corkers, flavoured as they are with the potent Source liquid. I highly rate these pellets and use the 3mm size in PVA bags and as a spod bait to lay down a bed of feed.

Naturals

This is probably the most ignored area of carp baits, and I can understand why. Using the large quantities of maggots, casters or worms needed in order to satisfy a large shoal of carp can be very expensive, and these particles don't tend to be instantly attractive or have a guaranteed response. I've used them on some waters where they were next to useless.

But on waters where the carp switch on to beds of maggots the feeding response has to be seen to be believed. On a highly pressured big carp water that had seen just about every carp bait known to man, I decided to spod out a large bed of maggots and fish two rods, tightly grouped over the top of them. For almost 48 hours nothing stirred. It was as if the maggots were totally lost on the carp. Then a fish crashed on the surface over the bait – it was a prelude to one of the most spectacular carp displays I've ever witnessed, and over the next four or five hours I caught three big carp and my swim turned into a fizzing maelstrom of carp activity.

An experienced carp angler who's been on the scene for decades stood open-mouthed in my swim as the water boiled with feeding activity. The carp were utterly preoccupied with mopping up every last grub. The only shame was that I soon ran out of bait and had to leave the water to go to work!

Maggots are a particularly great particle bait in winter when small fish activity is reduced and carp prefer picking up these smaller offerings. A great tip with maggots in the colder months is to use a mix of live and dead maggots. The dead maggots tend to be almost buoyant, and in the clear winter water provide a visual stimulus to complement the movement of the live ones.

Finally, on naturals, many a wary carp has been fooled by a big, fat, juicy lobworm. After heavy rain, naturals like worms end up being washed into the margins … so what could be more natural, and, fished just off the rod end under a float, what could be more exciting?

DIY or ready-prepared?

As already mentioned, preparing your own particles isn't difficult, but there's also an alternative option. These days several top bait companies sell ready-prepared particles. This provides you with a quick and easy way of 'flavouring the kitchen', and a superb backup to any session. Take them with you and have them handy, but you don't have to use them. If you don't think it's the right session just keep them for the next time. Part-used jars can be frozen, plus you can do all sorts of combinations. One of my favourites is a three-way mix of Hinders French Mix, Carp Crunch and hemp. You get a fabulous cloud of flavour in the water and loads of mini particles to keep the carp in your swim!

Ten great particle tips

1 Drill and balance

Use a Korda bait drill to remove a central plug of nut and then fill the hole with a small cork plug. This negates the weight of the hook and makes it far more likely that a carp will be hooked when it sucks up the bait.

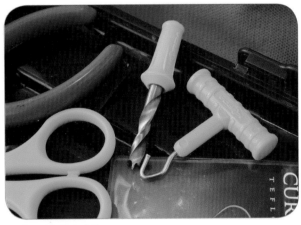

Korda or ESP bait drill.

With the bait drill you'll need a length of same-diameter cork dowel.

Carefully drill out the bait.

Push in the cork insert.

Ready to go … a proven top tactic!

Cut the cork to size.

Thread on to the hair. Either use a small shot or a second bait to balance.

2 Use a micromesh bag

Fill a fine-mesh PVA bag with maggots and attach it to your rig. If you're careful and don't pierce the maggots you can add the bag to the hook for casting, or you can attach a ring to the leger system and fix the bag to that. The hookbait can then be nicked into the bag to stop casting tangles.

4 Cut-down hookbaits

Linked to the tip above comes a cut-down hookbait that looks nothing like a whole tiger nut but still offers the smell and taste the carp crave. Remember, you often only have to change a bait slightly from the norm to give it a new lease of life.

3 Use chops

Place a handful of tiger nuts in a Korda Krusha and blitz them into a mass of small pieces. These bits of nut are then dried off or the moisture is blotted off with fishmeal groundbait until the nuts can be loaded inside a PVA bag without melting it. This is an awesome little edge on waters where the fish have been caught on whole tigers, as they don't suspect bits that look like they've passed through a carp's digestive tract.

5 Tie a chain

Tie a small metal rig on to a length of soft braid and attach it to a hook to form a hair rig. Position the ring tight to the back of the hookshank. Thread around ten maggots on a fine sewing needle and transfer them to a piece of floss or thin braid. Tie the line tightly to the ring – it'll be drawn down to form a ball of grubs that's hugely attractive.

6 Soak in oil

If you're using pellets as a hookbait, soak them in a light, perhaps flavoured, oil. It slows the breakdown rate of the pellet, which gives your hookbait a longer effective fishing time in the water.

7 Mount lengthways

A maize hookbait is far more visible to a passing carp if it's mounted lengthways on a hair rather than the more traditional side-on position. This can make a difference in clear water especially, and can get you extra bites in winter when the water often goes gin clear.

8 Target bait

I've mentioned using 'target baits' in the boilie chapter, and I use the same tactic when baiting with mass particles. If I'm putting down a bed of hemp, mini pellets or Partiblend, I usually use a small boilie or piece of maize on the hooklink and scatter a few samples of the hookbait in with the tiny feed baits.

9 Be different

When you're fishing a water, closely observe what baits other anglers are using. I'd hazard a guess that 95%-plus are only using boilies and pellets. This gives you the chance to use something different, at least on one rod. If nobody is

using maize or tigers then I often have one rig baited with those. It's amazing how often that bait is the first to rattle off.

10 Use rubber grubs

Using a rubber maggot to mask part of the hook is often referred to as the 'Mag-Aligner' rig. Positioning the buoyant rubber maggot over the eye of the hook helps to counteract the weight of the hook. It also creates an angle in the hook length, as it exits the rubber maggot, which helps the hook point turn and catch in the fish's mouth. At its simplest just position the rubber maggot over the eye/knot and add two or three live maggots directly onto the hook. For a larger mouthful, incorporate a small ring and attach a chain (Page 104). I often add a buoyant fake grub or two to the chain of live maggots tied to the ring as this also helps negate the weight of the hook.

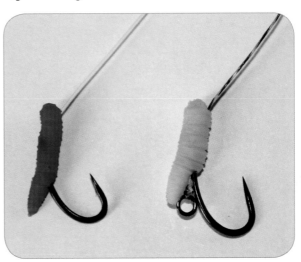

SETTING UP

Picking the right swim and being organised are essential parts of successful carping.

the water and organise yourself to fish efficiently. Unfortunately this is a crucial phase to which many carp anglers – even some experienced ones – pay far too little attention.

A flash new bite alarm, a new bait or the latest wonder-rig won't necessarily catch you more fish, but if you pick the right swim and put yourself 'on fish' the chances of success are instantly stacked in your favour.

In this chapter we deal with the basics of watercraft and what you could term 'swim management' – namely, how you organise yourself by the water. If you get these two elements correct then you'll move a long way down the road to catching carp.

Let's start with the biggest single factor that will dictate whether you catch fish and how many you bag.

You're now armed with the knowledge you need to choose and make bait, pick the right kit and create a rig that will cope with different situations. Now comes the hard bit – putting it all into practice!

The first step is to pick the right swim, set up your kit by

Choosing the right swim

Here's a quick test for you. Imagine a carp lake with a car park at one end and 20 pegs dotted equidistantly around the circumference. Now imagine a carp angler turns up to fish. Which swim do you think he'll pick?

The correct answer to this question should be that you've no idea where he'll fish. Without knowing an awful lot more about the lake, the features under and in the water, weather conditions and how he's geared up to tackle the venue, you can't possibly make a call on where that angler will pitch his gear.

Yet amazingly if you surveyed many carp lakes and selected the most popular swims I'd place a bet that the swims nearest the car park will almost certainly be among the most popular. The simple fact is that many anglers don't think hard about swim choice. Instead they often just 'drop in' the most accessible swims.

This is no way to go carp fishing. Clichéd it might be, but with the best tackle, rig and bait in the world, if you put it in the wrong place you won't catch many carp. So in this part of the book I'm going to provide guidance to selecting the best swim. But it's important you realise that such advice can only go so far, and the fact is you'll have to learn much of this art by trial and error.

You never stop learning when you go carp fishing, and one of the key things you constantly have to evaluate is, where should you fish? Successful carpers tend to make the right decision more often than not, and in my mind the best

A place where you can fish near the car is often popular … but not always the best choice.

sign you're becoming a more accomplished carp angler is making the right swim choice more frequently.

You won't always get it right. Carp are wild animals, and no matter how well we think we know them they do have a habit of doing the unexpected. This is one of the great things about carp fishing, and one of the high points for a fisherman is making a decision based on a 'gut' instinct that proves to be bang on. When you start to think like a carp you're well on your way to being a good carp angler.

So, how do you kick things off by picking the right swim?

Weather plays a part

The most obvious variable factor affecting fish behaviour and location is the weather. While it's impossible to make concrete rules for how fish will behave according to the weather, there are a few general principles that will stand you in good stead.

For a start carp usually feed best in warm or mild conditions, and are likely to be most active on days when a warm wind is blowing. As a general guide carp are instinctively programmed to follow a new wind direction if it's warm or mild; in contrast they'll usually ignore a cold wind or one that's been blowing in the same direction for several days.

In the warmer months, from April to November, the breeze is one of the biggest suppliers of natural food, and a warm wind that encourages flies to hatch will provide fish with plenty of natural food to follow. This behaviour is even more prominent if the wind is a strong one that sets up powerful wave action. Turbulence provides cover for carp, and a big southerly or south-westerly wind provides one of the golden opportunities for catching carp.

A new westerly or south-westerly wind that sends waves lapping into the northern and eastern sides of a lake is likely to carry carp with it – certainly in the warmer months of the year, and even in winter. Picking a swim with a new, mild wind pushing towards it is usually a good idea.

By contrast a cold easterly will drive fish away from the western bank, and in these conditions you often find fish move to the calm water on the eastern side or in the deeper centre portion of the lake. Picking a swim giving you casting access to this sheltered water is what's referred to as 'fishing on the back of the wind'.

Temperature also plays a part, and in warm conditions fish often feed high in the water column or on the surface. When it's really hot feeding might only take place on the bottom during the cool of night, and fish may even seek areas giving shade from the heat. Picking a swim containing plenty of weed, reeds, lilies or large overhanging trees may be a good option in these conditions. The fish also visit areas of shallow water, and swims in these areas often come good in summer.

In contrast, during the winter months carp spend most of

Long, hot spells can produce tricky conditions, so look for areas that get a breeze if there are any. Perhaps look for a swim near weeds, lily beds or overhanging trees providing shade.

their time in deeper areas where the temperature of the water is more stable and they find it more comfortable. That's not to say carp will always feed on the bottom in these swims. In some venues they'll actually feed in mid-water when it's cold; it's just that they prefer to have at least 4ft of water above them most of the time. Look for relatively deep areas of water in winter.

The exception to this rule comes on those rare days that are bright and relatively mild. On such occasions the fish may venture into shallower water just to feel the sun on their backs, and a short window of opportunity opens up before they retreat to deeper water.

Rain can have a positive or negative impact on the feeding behaviour of carp. After a long dry spell the eventual break in the weather is likely to herald a feeding binge as the rain invigorates the water by injecting fresh oxygen into it. This is especially the case if the rain is driven in by a strong, mild wind that puts a chop on the surface. In these circumstances move heaven and earth to get to the lake and get in a swim where the wind and rain is pushing into your face – the chances are carp will be galloping towards you.

The flip side to this comes with cold rain that's dumped from the skies over several days. Driven on by a northerly or easterly airstream, this rain is likely to chill the water and reduce feeding activity. Once again the fish are likely to back off from the direction of the wind or will seek the cover of deep water or snags on the sheltered side of the lake.

Winter can be hard going, but carp are still catchable.

Warm rain can improve sport in the summer. Cold rain in winter can chill the water and turn fish off.

Gravel bars can be obvious features that provide all sorts of fishing opportunities, from a bait placed on top for fish passing over, to down the sides, where food collects.

Look for features

Later in this chapter we'll look at how you use a marker float to locate sub-surface features such as bars or humps, weed beds, depth drop-offs and changes in the make-up of the lake bed. All of these obstructions can influence your choice of swim. But other features are more obvious. Islands, beds of weed, reeds and lily pads, as well as overhanging trees and bushes, all provide sanctuary and are often a source of food too. These great features should never be ignored.

Weed beds provide food and shade.

Pads can look like a jungle, but under the leaves there are often clear routes that fish follow. Just make sure your gear is up to the job.

Islands can be a magnet for carp as they circle them looking for feeding opportunities.

Carp will be happy in this environment, but where does the angler start?

Swims that give casting access to areas like this can be so-called 'bankers' that you can fall back on if you don't see signs of life elsewhere. Carp spend a lot of time tucked into weed and under trees, and casting near to these fish-holding features is often a sure-fire way to catch carp.

The effects of angling pressure

The activity of other anglers is almost impossible to predict but it can have a significant impact on the carp's feeding behaviour. On every lake I've ever fished the carp get harder to catch when there's a lot of bank-side disturbance and noise. If anglers adjacent to you are hammering bivvy pegs into the ground or shouting to a mate across the lake they'll probably make things more difficult for you too, as they'll alert the carp to the presence of anglers.

The flip side of this is when you arrive on a busy lake and spend some time searching for wherever the fish have

tucked themselves away to get away from the disturbance. I can think of many occasions when I've caught fish simply because I've picked a swim well away from the crowds.

On one lake I fish I purposely don't turn up until mid-morning on Saturday when most of the swims are occupied by anglers bivvied up for a couple of days. Experience has taught me that a group of fish will have scooted out of the main body of the lake into a quiet corner where there are no proper swims and no anglers. Then I creep into the corner with a single rod, lower a rig near the edge of an overhanging tree and often catch a carp within an hour. It's simply a case of picking a specific swim that fishes well when the lake is busy.

Expect the unexpected!

I've now given you a number of rules or general principles that should be taken into consideration before you pick your swim. If you bear them in mind and then spend plenty of time walking round the lake – looking carefully for signs of carp activity, such as rolling fish, bubbling or coloured water – you should put yourself on fish more often than you pick a 'duff' swim.

Using your eyes to find fish can make a huge difference to what you catch. Just one fish sighting can make the difference between catching lots and blanking. One November I saw a single carp poke its head out of the water in a very unusual position that I'd never seen anyone cast anywhere near. I acted on the sighting and quickly got a rod on the spot. Over the next four days' fishing, spread over two weeks, I fished one rod in the area and had five carp from there, including a 41-pounder. My other two rods produced just one fish between them in the same time.

Then there are the times when the carp will behave totally bizarrely – it goes freezing cold and they have a feeding binge, a big south-westerly blows up and the fish get caught on the back of the wind etc.

Personally I don't get wound up by such crazy occurrences. I take it as a lesson to remember and literally put it down to experience. I might have caught nothing and another angler might have had five, but if I've added to my bank of knowledge and learned to recognise the signs of this happening in the future then I've become a better carp angler in the process of not catching anything!

Use your eyes and move if you are not on the fish.

A walk around the lake: picking where to fish

So, let's take a walk round the fictitious carp lake in the accompanying plan. It's late summer, the weather is warm and sunny with a gentle south-west wind.

1 The car park bank
Usually busy swims, and the area is consequently nicknamed 'the social bank'. The gravel bar to the left of the car park bank used to produce well in response to single baits and small bags, but in the last year or so fish have become very nervous and takes have become few and far between. The last swim on the left of the car park bank can be a good stalking swim, fishing just off the reeds. The other end of the car park bank can still produce well, particularly with a north-west wind, but you have to lock the clutch down and sit close to your rods, as the fish usually try to make it into the weeds.

2 Walking along the east bank
There's a great stalking swim just after you get round the corner. Fish regularly come out of the main weed bed and move along the margin. I love dropping a bit of bait here and keeping an eye on it. When I see fish in the area it's time for one rod and some under-the-rod top action.

The main swim on this bank is a cracker, because you have so many options. A gravel bar in front, weed beds and pads to your right and some open water to the left, so whatever the weather or time of year you have tactical options. It's also a fair walk from the car park, so the gravel bar isn't as pressured as the one near there.

3 Walking along the north bank
Although it's a long walk from the car park, this is my favourite bank. All four swims give me options. In summer the stream brings fresh, oxygenated water, and it's a real holding area.

The first swim fishes short left to the edge of the pads. In the summer fish spend a lot of time there, coming out at night to feed. The middle rod fishes longer off the weed bed, and the right-hand rod goes along the treeline to the right.

The middle swim is all hit and hold, with baits fished long, close to the central pads, and left or right to the island margins. You have to clip up and get your cast right, but fish spend a lot of time there, so you're always in with a chance. The open water can also fish well, particularly in the colder months. The near margins left and right are also very good, especially if there's no one else on the bank with you.

The other two swims as you head to the corner are great short-session swims, fishing close in off the reeds or to along the overhanging trees. These are also good colder-weather swims fishing the deeper open water.

4 Walking along the west bank
The middle gravel bar swim on this bank is another swim with plenty of tactical options, but it isn't a particularly popular swim as the extensive reed beds either side extend a long way out into

the water, and a lot of fish get snagged up. You need strong gear and muscles if you're going to have a good chance of landing fish you hook here. In the winter, when the weed beds have died back, the deeper water left and right can produce well.

5 The south-west corner

This corner always looks better than it actually is. Fish don't seem to favour it – perhaps because the wind that blows into this corner is usually a cold one, and it's a very shallow area. I only fish this as a stalking area when I can see that fish are active here.

I've had my walk round, so it's decision time

Today I'm going on the north bank first swim nearest the pads and the stream. With the nice weather and the gentle south-westerly there are stacks of fish in the corner weeds and pads, so I fancy my chances using the breeze to drift floaters into them and, later in the evening, I should get a take or two on the bottom as they come out for a scoff!

Time for the trolley...

Organising your swim

One of the key skills that's most often overlooked is how to organise yourself on the bank. Basically, if you fish efficiently, with everything placed thoughtfully in the right spot, then you're much more likely to fish effectively.

The photographs across these two pages show how I typically lay out my rods, bivvy and equipment when I go fishing. Everything is ordered, and I try to place my kit in exactly the same place every time I go fishing. Why? Well, when you wake up to a run in the middle of the night you probably won't be at your sharpest for a few seconds, and it makes sense for you to know instinctively where all the kit you need will be. The last thing you want to be doing is scrambling around for your shoes or head torch as your bite alarm wails in the background!

You don't have to organise your swim in the same way that I do – you may have a system that works better for you. But the point is that you must have a system. An ordered swim is an efficient swim.

Rods

Ideally I place mine on single bank sticks, as they allow each rod to be pointed directly at the bait for better bite registration. They're also more stable than a rod pod. That said, on hard ground or a platform peg I have no hesitation using a pod. I place my rods to one side of the swim to leave a large space to play and land the fish.

Net

This is placed by the water to the open side of the swim, ready to land a fish. It might sound a bit flash, but if the water you're fishing is prolific think about having two nets – it's surprising how often you get a second run before the first fish has been returned.

Bivvy

This is placed to the side of the rods but turned at an angle that enables you to see the water where you've cast your rods, even when you're lying in your sleeping bag. Just make sure the bivvy isn't in the way of where you need to drop the leger to cast. I use either a Fox Royale or a Nash Titan bivvy in which I've spent more nights than any other.

Bedchair

Don't skimp on a poor-quality bed you can't sleep on. It'll soon make you feel exhausted and you'll fish badly. I love the Nash Indulgence range. Although they're big and heavy, they're wonderfully comfortable, solid and, most importantly (for me at any rate), they lie flat. I place my bedchair so that I can see the water I'm fishing even when I'm tucked up inside the sleeping bag.

Sleeping bag

It's got to keep you warm, be wide enough to stretch over your bivvy and needs to have 'crash zips' that'll burst open when you get a take.

Head torch

An invaluable piece of kit that always hangs off the ratchet of the bedchair, so that I can put my hand on it even in the pitch darkness.

Cooking kit

This must always be stored and used outside the bivvy so that it poses no risk to the angler. Bivvies are extremely flammable, and the fumes off a burning stove can prove lethal in a confined space.

Tackle box

I store my Korum Intelligent Tackle Manager box under the bedchair so that I can place my hand on it in an instant when I need a replacement hooklink or an item of end tackle. I leave key items of kit – like baiting needles, boilie stops and lighter – on top of the box.

Rucksack

I store all the other bits and pieces that I carry, such as spares, PVA, food and clothing, in a Nash Boxlogix Cube or carryall that I stow under my bedchair.

Sounder box

If you've got a bite alarm set that has one, place the sounder box right under your bedchair, or drop it into a purpose-made pocket like this, which is tucked inside the Fox Royale bivvy. A simple idea, but it ensures that the sounder box is hanging right above your head.

Bait bag

I pack my bait inside the purpose-made panniers that slot on to the side of my Nash Trax Evolution trolley. It's then an easy job to unclip the bag and place it under the bedchair. Inside the bag I keep my PVA and catapults as well as the spare baits.

Feature finding

Now we come to one of the most important skills to learn, which will set you on the road to catching carp – finding features that are hidden below the water.

Every lake has features of some description below the water. In ancient meres you'll have to map out a silty basin where the only 'features' you're likely to find are areas of firmer silt or small deviations in depth. By contrast gravel pits that have been man-made in the last 50 years can have an egg-box style topography, with steep gravel bars, wide plateaux and deep gullies.

The sequence below provides a step-by-step guide to how you find features below the water using a marker float set-up. Once you've drawn up a picture of what's below the surface on lakes that you visit frequently you'll find that you

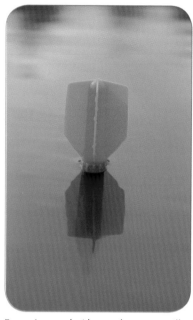

Becoming good with a marker set-up will help you establish what conditions are like beneath the surface, and will help you catch more fish.

need to use the marker float less and less, which will reduce the disturbance you make in your swim.

Marker floats allow you to learn an awful lot about the fisheries you visit, and using them will make your fishing and baiting-up operations more accurate. Here's how you do it…

The kit you need

There are dozens of purpose-made marker rods available, which boast a specially beefed-up action that allows you to cast a heavy leger and float a long way.

But strong though these rods are, they also have a slightly softer tip that allows you to feel the make-up of the lake bed – is it soft and silty, hard and gravelly, or strewn with weed? The tip will help tell you determine this information, especially if you use it with a reel loaded with super-thin braid that has virtually zero stretch. In fact to use a marker float efficiently you *must* use braid on the reel rather than nylon monofilament. Companies like Nash, Fox and E-S-P produce purpose-made braid that helps register every bump on the bottom. That's why E-S-P's marker braid is called Sonar, as it allows you to read the make-up of the lake bed very accurately.

When you cast out the float you want to launch it tight to the line clip, then feel the leger down to the lake bed on a tight line. If it lands with a hard thump you know you've hit gravel. By contrast, if it makes a soft landing then the bottom is silty or muddy, while if it makes a spongy, almost indiscernible touchdown then you know you've found weed.

Repeatedly measuring the depth of the water in this way, and allowing your leger to bump across the lake bed and register its make-up, enables you to gradually chart your swim.

Here's how you use a marker float set-up:

A good-quality, beefy marker rod is an essential, as a marker won't cast as easily as the rig will.

A fully loaded, large-capacity reel also helps.

Using a marker float

1 There are lots of great marker float set-ups available from companies like Nash and Korda. This is my favourite, the Fox Exocet. The float casts for miles, is very buoyant and it's easy to pull the line through the large ring on the end of the leger link.

2 The large ring helps the line go through it, and the buoyant ball helps keep the link off the bottom so that it doesn't get weeded up.

3 The shape of the lead helps pick out features on the bottom.

4 I also carry more buoyant floats for use in heavily weeded waters where smaller floats get bound up in weed. This is the Nash weed marker. Made of foam, it's so buoyant that it pulls through weed to rise to the surface.

5 This diagram shows how the set-up works.

STAGES IN USING A MARKER FLOAT

Lead landed with a definite 'donk' so you know you're on hard ground, possibly gravel. Tighten the line to the lead, then pull line off a foot at a time until you know the depth.

Re-tighten the line to the lead and pull it towards you. This time you can feel the lead catching on weed. Again find the depth, but pulling line off a foot at a time

Re-tighten again and pull it a bit closer. Still catching weed, but this time it is shallower, you are obviously on some sort of weed covered bar.

Re-tighten and pull closer again, you feel it roll towards you a bit and another slight pull feels sluggish and softer. Letting the float up it's getting deeper again so you might have found a silt pocket at the bottom of a small gravel bar.

6 Cast out and then wind down the line so that the float pulls against the leger.

7 Slacken off the clutch so that you can pull line off the reel easily.

8 Pull line off the reel a foot at a time. Most marker rods have a band on the rod 6in and/or 12in from the reel.

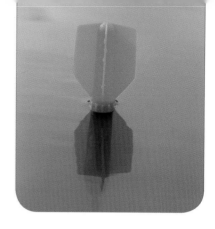

9 Keep pulling line off the reel, counting how many feet of line you have to release off the reel to allow the float to surface.

10 Pull the float back down to the leger, bounce it across the bottom, and repeat steps six and seven to record the depth across the swim.

11 As you pull the float towards the bank, sweep the rod to the left or right before you tighten up to the leger and then let the float up again. This allows you to feel the texture of the bottom as you bring the leger in.

12 Repeat the process several times in a wide sweep from one side of the swim to the other. This will allow you to build up a picture of the entire lake bed.

13 Once you've located the spot you want to fish, slip the line into the clip on the reel to set your casting distance.

14 Now you set the casting distance of your fishing rods, and if needed your spod rod (more about spod rods later). One option is to lay out the float and rig side-by-side on the bank then walk down the bank until you hit the clip on the marker rod. The fishing rod and spod rod are then clipped up at that point. As long as you make a note of far bank markers on the skyline (so you can re-cast accurately at night), the float can be retrieved yet you can still cast accurately.

15 Better still you can record the actual casting distance using two bank sticks. Simply lay the rod on the ground and place a bank stick at either end – they're then 12ft apart.

16 Now lay midway between the two sticks, wrap the float around one of them and whip the line round the two sticks, counting how many turns it takes until you hit the clip.

17 Once you've recorded how far out the marker float was clipped up you simply wrap the line on your fishing rods round the sticks to the same number of turns, then clip up. This has the advantage of allowing you to simply stake out the bank sticks the next time you fish the swim and repeat the process to clip the line at the same point.

18 Mark your line at the casting distance by tying a piece of thin pole elastic or marker elastic to the mainline just beyond the rod tip when the line is tight to the clip. When you then cast out, the sight (and sound) of the elastic rattling through the rod rings will alert you to the fact that the line is about to hit the clip.

Tying a pole elastic marker

1 Cut off a short length of pole marker elastic.

2 Form it into a loop next to your mainline.

3 Thread one end of the elastic through the loop and around the line four times.

4 Gently pull both ends to start to tighten the knot.

5 Moisten the knot and pull tight.

6 Trim off both ends.

7 You have a completed marker knot. To remove, just hold the mainline and pull one end of the marker knot sharply.

Why does it matter?

Using a marker float is a technique that many anglers just don't bother with, but this is a great shame as it means you're fishing 'blind' – you don't know what's below the water and you certainly have no idea of any hidden features that may influence carp's movements.

As you get to know a venue you can gradually use a marker float less often to map the topography of the lake bed. This reduces the chance of spooking fish by repeatedly hitting the surface with the leger and float. But in the early stages of fishing on a new water a marker float tells you many things of which you'd otherwise be ignorant. Depth drop-offs, for example, often act as fish highways. Carp move along shelves and channels just like cars run along roads, and often move from one part of the lake to another along these distinct routes. A marker float helps locate these pathways. In fact ANY underwater feature can be a carp magnet at one time or another, and the important thing is that you know where these deviations are.

Once you've got this knowledge you can start to work out where fish are likely to move, and if you do see a fish roll on the surface you can make an educated guess on exactly where the fish are feeding or moving. Your ability to read the water and the carp's movement is massively enhanced when you've mapped the shape of the lake bed.

Casting out

You're now ready to make your play for a carp by casting your baited rig into the water. The sequence below shows how you launch your rig accurately to put it where you want it, and how you set your indicators on the line to register a bite.

It's imperative you follow a routine with your casting, as once you slot into a rhythm you'll find you hit the spot you want first time more of the time. Limiting the number of casts you make reduces the disturbance you create and decreases the chance of spooking fish feeding near your baited area.

Making one cast is so much better than making two or three, and it's small things like casting accurately that will do so much to increase your catches.

1 Bait your rig and retrieve the line until the leger hangs 4–6ft below the tip. This allows smoother casting and enables you to compress the rod better.

2 Find a comfortable standing position and make a note of exactly where it is, so that you can repeat the cast again later, hopefully after you've caught your first fish!

3 Open the bale arm on the reel to release the line into the crook in your first finger. Hold the line tight to the spool to stop it pouring off the reel.

4 Swing the rod directly over your head, lining it up between your eyes and the far bank marker/tree/feature that you've picked to target.

5 Sweep the rod forward, generating casting power in the rod and launching the leger at its target. Release the line as the rod reaches the ten o'clock position.

11 Engage your freespool system or slacken the drag system so it will release line if a carp picks up the bait, is hooked and charges off.

12 Lay the rod across the bite alarm and rear rod rest, with the first rod ring ideally placed 10–12in behind the alarm.

6 Hold the rod vertically in the air as the leger flies out and the line pours off the reel. Hover your finger about the line peeling off the open spool.

7 As the line is about to pull into the clip, the elastic marker pulls off the spool and rattles through the rod rings. Feather the line with your finger to slow the leger.

8 When the line pulls tight into the line clip smoothly lower the rod, keeping the line tight to cushion the lead on to the water. That way it kisses the water rather than slamming into it.

9 The leger hits the water on a tight line right on the mark you want it, and because it's been slowed down the hooklink is laid out across the surface, avoiding tangles.

10 Unclip the line from the spool's line-clip and carefully take up any remaining slack, making sure not to move the lead. It's a good idea to lower the rod top to make sure all the spare line is back on the reel.

13 Attach the bite indicator to the line. Some anglers like the line bowstring tight, others pull off enough line to allow a small drop to hang down from the alarm.

14 You can pull so much line off the reel that it sinks and lays on the lake bed, and the bite indictor hangs slack. Wary fish find it harder to spot and be alerted by the line.

You're ready for action

And that's it. The baited rigs are out and you're fishing – will the carp read the script and come to the party?

Well, they might, if you bait up your swim with free offerings to attract and feed them. In the next chapter we'll look at what can be done to prepare a swim properly, since applying bait intelligently can make a massive difference to what you catch.

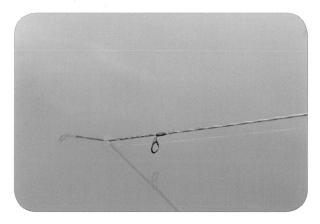

BAITING UP

Feeding your swim with free bait for fish to settle on to feed is one of the foundations of a successful carp fishing session. In fact an angler who can feed his swim accurately with the right bait is almost always holding the key to making a catch.

In this chapter I'll look at techniques for baiting and strategies for how you bait up your swim to attract carp to it. Often overlooked, this is one of the most important chapters in this book, because how you apply bait has a direct impact on what you catch.

Before we get into the finer detail of equipment and how bait is applied, here are a few quick pointers regarding how to apply bait.

First decide what job the bait you use is going to do. Yes, we know it's meant to get the carp feeding, but how is it going to achieve this? For example, if your water is lightly stocked with fish, weather conditions are poor or the fishery is heaving with other anglers you might need to be conservative with the amount of bait you feed. If carp aren't feeding strongly or there are mountains of baits lying all over the fishery competing for the fish's attention, just piling yet more bait into the swim is unlikely to be a great way to catch fish.

In this case a smaller food supply, where you limit the free offerings to the fish, will focus their attention on your bait. This situation might even be the sort of day when a high-attract single hookbait (*ie* a baited rig and no free offerings) is the best way to earn a pickup.

The flip side of this is when conditions are running in your favour. A mild day with rough, windy weather, low angler pressure and a healthy stock of fish are all factors that will encourage fish to feed and you to bait up more positively. The fact is, the carp are likely to be feeding strongly and (within reason) this is the sort of day where the more bait you apply the more you'll catch.

Let's turn our attention now to the methods with which you bait up and how much bait you apply.

Methods of baiting up

1 The catapult

The traditional way to bait up a swim is with a catapult, and I carry a range of catties that serve me well. My personal favourites are the catapults made by Drennan and Fox. I haven't used catapults made by any other company for years and can confidently recommend them.

I really like the Groundbait Feederpults from Drennan.

The catties I use for 75% of my fishing are the groundbait catapults made by Drennan, originally designed for firing out balls of groundbait when bream fishing. I find the pouch and elastic is absolutely ideal for creating a tight grouping of boilies.

The green version with the softer elastic is used for shorter ranges of 40 yards or less; three boilies will land in a close grouping. At ranges of less than 30 yards up to ten small boilies can be fired with fabulous accuracy.

For longer mid-range fishing of 40–60 yards the stronger red version (medium latex) has stronger elastic to deliver baits with great accuracy. As long as you don't overload the pouch and only fire in three boilies at a time they'll fly in a neat pattern, landing just a foot or so apart. With repeated baiting you can soon lay down a bed of bait in a tight area that draws fish to your baited rig.

When it comes to long-range fishing of up to 90 yards Drennan's Boiliepult is my choice. Although it's old I like the sturdy frame, and replace the pouch with the smaller Scruffy Bob pouches (see pic on right) sold by Kent's Tackle Box fishing shop. With this catty I fire in three boilies at a time or, for maximum range fishing, I'll load one bigger bait of 18mm into the pouch and fire that. I've got used to using the catty and can quickly bait up at long range with great accuracy.

In recent times I've started using Fox's catties and have to say I'm impressed with them. I particularly like the Fox Power Guard complete with hand guard to stop the elastic and

The Fox Power Guard catty is my favourite for long range.

catty pouch rapping your knuckles and taking the skin off. It's a neat idea, and would be even better if it had a wrist support to take even more of the strain.

Before we move off catapults I've got to mention a few key pointers to using them. First, always have plenty of spare elastics and pouches, because the simple fact is these aren't built to provide long service. Elastics soon wear out, and repeatedly cutting off the worn-out end is no solution: it reduces the maximum range of the 'pult and actually changes the 'action' of the elastics. I'll snip mine once or twice at most, then it's in the bin and on with new ones.

Second, take great care to ensure that the elastics are both exactly the same length, and that the pouch is hanging straight down and isn't twisting. Uneven laccies or pouches that spin and twist are a recipe for poor distance. It's also more likely the baits will group poorly and will fly off at wild angles. Straight, untwisted elastics of even length produce the best accuracy.

Always have plenty of spare elastics.

2 The throwing stick

I have to make an admission here. I don't like throwing sticks. I find it difficult to produce what I would consider an accurate baiting pattern, and I just don't like the lack of control a stick gives compared to the tension-loading you can actually feel in catty elastic. I've watched many self-proclaimed 'experts' bait up with a throwing stick, and I

The throwing stick – not my favourite, but some carpers love them and can achieve huge distances with them.

don't believe I couldn't have produced a neater, more accurate baiting pattern with a catapult.

However, fans of sticks will doubtless say my viewpoint is explained by my simply not being very good with them, and they do have a point. Friends of mine who are very successful carpers are also very good with a stick, so I do see that they have a place in carp fishing. So my lack of faith in them shouldn't be taken as the only view.

The situation in which I can see them being most effective (and the only time I use them) is when fishing at extreme range. The simple fact is that a throwing stick puts a boilie further out than a catapult can. An 18mm or 20mm bait that's been specially hardened by extra cooking, more drying or by the addition of ingredients that toughen up the bait during cooking, will fly a long, long way if you use a throwing stick correctly.

The key to maximising distance and accuracy is building up a rhythm. Strap a boilie pouch round your waist so you don't need to bend down to pick up baits, and deliver them with a flicking action from the elbow and wrist rather than the shoulder. Wetting the inside of the stick can also help them fly further, as it reduces the friction and the chance of the baits splitting as they're fired out of the hollow stick.

Using the stick double-handed so that it's fired directly over your head generates even more power, and is a special skill that takes extra practice but is well worth working at for delivering baits at maximum range. Master this technique and you'll put big boilies over 100 yards out.

3 The spod

This is my favourite way to bait up at long range or to feed small baits (such as pellets and hemp) that simply can't be fired a long way accurately by catapult.

A spod is the common name for a bait rocket, which is simply a plastic tube filled with bait and cast into the water where you want it. The spod's buoyant nosecone tips it upside down, and as it sits upright on the surface the payload of bait drops out below, spreading out in a narrow cone. It's a very effective way to bait your swim with lots of bait quickly and (with practice) accurately. It also allows you to place small baits, groundbait or even sloppy feeds at far greater distances than you'd ever achieve with a catapult.

Spodding accurately is a great skill, and the following sequence shows you how to do it:

Spodding ... my favourite way to bait up at long range.

1 The first thing you've got to do is get a specialist spod rod that's been specially strengthened for the job. I use a Bruce Ashby Rocketeer. It's a powerful rod sold by The Tackle Box shop in Kent, but it's not a poker-style rod that doesn't bend, like some spod rods I've tried. While this might not be the best option for extreme-range fishing, I've personally never fished at a distance that I can't cast a spod with this rod.

2 The rod must be matched with an equally beefy reel that's going to be up to the task of repeatedly launching out a fully-laden spod and pulling it back through the water. A Daiwa Emblem Exceler, like all the big pit-style reels produced by this company, features powerful gearing, great line lay and a spool that's big enough to comfortably accommodate the powerful braid I use for spodding.

3 This brings me neatly on to the line itself, and you'll see I use braid for this. The lack of stretch in braid means that more of the casting power is funnelled directly down to the spod. This results in longer and more accurate casting. I would *never* spod with monofilament line. Instead I use a shock leader where I fill the reel with fine diameter 20lb Berkley Whiplash Pro braid before attaching a length of 30lb or 50lb Korda Arma Cord. This super-tough braid takes the shock of the cast.

Take your two lines, the lighter mainline/braid and the heavier shock leader braid.

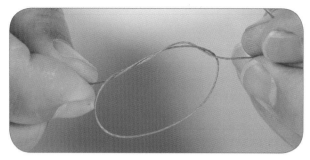

Make a loop in the heavier braid and pass the end through it twice.

Gently pull it together so it forms a small figure of eight. This might cause the fibres of the braid to open a bit, but this isn't a problem – they'll close back up later in the process.

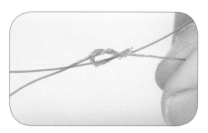

Pass the lighter line/braid through the two halves of the figure of eight...

...then close the figure of eight by pulling on the tag end.

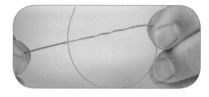

Hold the knot in one hand and use the other to twist the lighter line/braid around the heaver braid. Tuck the end back through the gap nearest the knot.

Do five more turns back through the loop and up the heavier braid.

Moisten and tease the light line/braid knot tight, up the heavier leader braid.

Moisten and bring the two knots together.

4 I use the leader knot for tying the two lines together. (For picture sequence purposes I've used Sensor mono instead of the whiplash, so that they contrast in the pictures.) Having tied the two braids together I wind five or six turns of the Arma Cord on to the reel. This takes the strain (the 'shock') of the cast. The spod is then tied on the other end. I use enough braid so that the line runs through the rod rings and down to almost the halfway point in the rod. This long drop between spod and rod tip helps to generate and use the full power of the rod to get maximum casting performance.

Trim off both tag ends.

This will produce a very compact and very strong leader knot.

5 Before you start casting the spod it's essential to get the line clipped up at the required distance so that each payload of bait lands in the same spot. Do this by casting the spod out to a marker float over the spot you want to hit, then clip up the line. Alternatively lay your rig and marker float beside each other on the ground, open the bale arms on both reels and walk out the lines

until the rig line hits the clip. Slip the braid into the clip on the spodding set-up and you're ready to cast.

6 Now fill the spod with bait. The spod I use is the radically designed Spomb. Unlike all other spods, which are made out of a plastic tube that's open at one end, the Spomb is a bomb-shaped missile that opens in two at the press of a button on the nosecone. You fill half the spod with bait, making sure

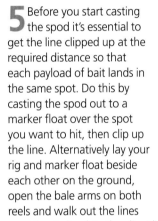

you leave the spring mechanism unobstructed, then snap it shut. The bait is fully enclosed within the frame of the spod, ready for casting out.

7 You then wind up the spod until five or six turns of the Arma Kord are wound on to the spool. This means that it'll be hanging almost halfway down the rod in

readiness to cast. Standing almost shoulder-on to the water, swing the spod back and forth a couple of times, then let rip with the cast when the spod is fully extending the back cast and the rod is being compressed behind you. The rod will compress and the spod will be fired out. I use a leather casting glove to stop the braid cutting into my finger.

8 The Spomb or spod flies out, and, thanks to the lack of stretch in the shock leader and the braided mainline, maximum casting performance is achieved. As the Spomb or spod flies through the air, lift the rod straight up in the air and feather the line with your

finger to slow it down just before it pulls into the line clip on the reel. As the braided line pulls tight to the clip, lower the rod in a smooth arc to drop the Spomb or spod, on a tight line, on to the water. It will then upend or open and deposit the bait.

THE SPOMB IN ACTION

The button on the front of the spomb releases the catch and the spomb springs open.

Use in conjuction with your market float to make sure all the bait is in the same area.

9 As this illustration and photograph demonstrate, the nosecone on the front of the Spomb includes a red button that's pushed in by impact with the water. This activates the spring release mechanism and the spod springs open, releasing its payload of bait right on target. This is one of the unique aspects of this spod design – not a single bait is spilt in flight, and every single bait is dumped on contact with the water.

10 Finally, you wind the spod back in for refilling. Thanks to the fact that line is attached to the rear of the Spomb where it opens, you end up pulling back a very water-dynamic spod that's so much easier and quicker to retrieve than other, more traditional designs. It skips across the surface rather than digging into the water. This makes it quicker to bait up with, as well as making it more efficient, with no spilt feed.

11 There are three different versions of the Spomb: a big one that carries lots of food, a smaller one that's half that size, and a mid-sized one. Personally I use the big one for producing big beds of bait very quickly, but I find the smaller one easier to use with maximum accuracy, so in most

of my spodding sessions this is the one I use. It's also effective when spodding floating baits and sloppy groundbait.

12 My favourite spodding recipe is a mixture of 3mm and 6mm Trigga Ice pellets, hemp seed, crushed boilies and whole baits to provide a match with the hookbait. It's also worth mentioning I put the bucket containing my bait on my trolley or on top of another bait bucket so that it's lifted off the ground and nearer to thigh level. This makes refilling the spod easier and speeds up the baiting process.

Different baiting tactics

This is a strangely neglected part of the carp-catching equation, as too many anglers are only bothered about *how* they bait up, and not *how much* they bait up with.

Giving someone advice on how much bait they should use is almost impossible, as weather conditions influence this decision, as does time of year and angler pressure. Nevertheless, there are a few general tactics that are essential to look at.

Single hookbaits

In simple terms this is when you don't add any free offerings to your swim but rely instead on the pulling power of the hookbait to do the job for you. This is a popular tactic, and it does produce a lot of carp, especially in winter and during periods of intense angling pressure, when creating minimum disturbance can make the difference between catching and not. I tend to use single hookbaits when casting to fish that are repeatedly showing on the surface, so that I don't spook them by making too much disturbance.

When I'm single-hookbait fishing I use a bait that's been loaded with an extra source of attraction, and I carry a range of boilies that have been doused in flavouring or extra attractors. I often tip my hookbaits with a piece of plastic corn soaked in Nash Sweetcorn extract, but I also carry a range of Solar pop-up boilies soaked in Pot Shots of the same flavour. Pop-ups are a favourite of mine when I'm fishing 'singles', as they stand out a little bit more. The Squid and Octopus boilies are a particular favourite of mine.

I'll mention one more of my special singles that I never go fishing without, namely Nutrabaits Tecni-spice boilies, soaked in 50ml of Bait Soak Complex, boosted with 3ml of Sweet Nutraspice flavour. I've had boilies soaked in this solution for almost ten years, and they just seem to keep getting better,

A single bait with a 'tippet' of plastic corn. A great tactic to use on fish you see topping.

I glug my plastic corn in Nash Sweetcorn extract.

I keep a range of plastic baits in the glug.

Solar pop-ups and Pot Shots, another of my favourite high attract options.

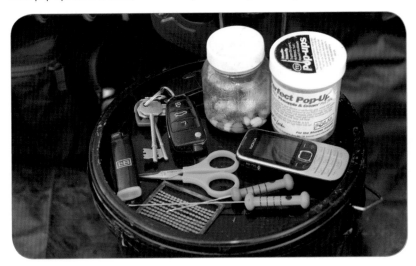

Glugged Tecni-spice, one of my favourite cold-water baits.

especially in the colder months from November through to early May. Because they've been soaking for so long they leak a trail of flavour for many hours.

Sparse baiting

This is a slight twist on fishing singles, as it gives the fish a tiny taster of free feed and advertises the hookbait without giving them much of a choice before they take the bait. This is one of my personal favourite ways to fish, especially when I'm on a short session and there isn't enough time to wait for a big baiting plan to pay off.

I use one of the high-attract boilies listed above as my hookbait, and marry it with a small PVA mesh bag packed with tiny pellets or a couple of crushed boilies or broken boilies. This addition of freebie pellets or boilies right next to the hookbait adds an extra source of attraction that advertises the bait that little bit more.

I'm a huge fan of this baiting tactic. It suits my fishing style and the shorter sessions I typically fish midweek or on quick overnight trips after work when I'm trying to pick up a bite or two and I'm not trying to empty the swim.

What I especially like about this style of baiting is that it's great at any time of the year, from the depths of winter through to high summer. It creates minimal disturbance, so bites can come soon after casting out.

Heavy baiting

This is a tactic to use when you think a red letter day is in the offing and your swim has large numbers of fish feeding avidly. Big beds of boilies, pellets, particles or combinations of all three can get a shoal feeding and hold them in your swim for several hours. I use this tactic in the warmer

months when the carp are especially up for feeding.

Beds of bait can be placed with catapult and throwing stick, but the common way to lay down a pile of feed is with a spod. I often use this tactic if I'm fishing for a couple of days or more, as it gives the fish time to find the bait and settle on it for a hearty feed.

Get it right and the pay-off with a heavy baiting tactic can be spectacular. On one trip I had to the Acton Burnell fishery a few years ago I did the first 24 hours of the session with one fish to show for my efforts while using a small bed of bait; that was a decent result but not an extravagant one. I didn't feel I was getting it completely right, and decided to go for it: I spent two hours spodding to deliver a deluge of Trigga pellets, hemp and boilies. For the next 24 hours nothing happened, but then chaos broke out. Lots of fish moved on to the bed of bait and I had 11 runs in 12 hours that brought me a 19-pounder, four 20s, five 30s and a 42-pounder.

The swim had all the elements a heavy baiting campaign needs to work – good weather, lots of fish, nobody else baiting up heavily, and the right swim where I could monopolise the bait I'd put in and didn't have to share it with other anglers who could cast to the same general area.

Obviously there are baiting plans that slot into the middle ground between heavy baiting and single hookbait fishing. Deciding how much bait to use tends to be a gut instinct that develops from experience.

It's impossible to say whether you should use a particular quantity of bait at a particular water – too much changes each time you go fishing. As a general rule you should consider the weather, angler pressure and the length of time you're spending on the bank. These are all variables, and the more you think about them the better.

Tight or spread out?

Now we have to consider how the baits are placed in the water. More specifically, do you pack them in a very small area or purposely spread them out?

Although it isn't fashionable to say so, I prefer to spread my bait over an area about the size of a couple of cars. This has a couple of major advantages over the more popular tightly placed bed that's grouped within a few yards square.

Sometimes just fishing for one bite is the best option, and a small PVA bag of crushed boilies or pellets can attract the fish to your hookbait.

In the right conditions heavy baiting with boilies, pellets or particles can produce multiple catches.

BAITING UP TACTICS

By spreading your bait out you increase your chances of attracting fish coming from different directions

Firstly, spreading the bait like this allows you to place two or even three rods on one baited area without dropping them virtually on top of each other. I often fish two rods within the centre section of the baited area and one several yards away just off it. In my mind it's a sign of getting things right when all your rods are producing bites and you're not sure which one's most likely to go next.

This strategy also allows your baited area to intercept more moving fish, as a wider area is covered. The diagram above shows how more fish are intercepted by the bait and how I'd typically cast the rods. As you can see, I stagger the hookbaits across the baited area to intercept more fish. In addition having a well-spread area like this reduces the risk of one hooked fish spooking the rest of its shoal mates. One run can then easily become two or three, and a multiple catch is on the cards.

The exception to this rule comes when there's a real

hotspot you're fishing to. It might be a small gravel hole in thick weed or a gap in a line of impenetrable snags that fish come in and out of. In such a specific case it can be best to cast your rig right into the lions' den and concentrate all your bait in a tight area. This is where your ability to accurately catapult your free offerings will be put to the test. Get it right and you'll have a neat patch of bait tightly clustered around a rig in the middle of the feeding hotspot. Get it wrong and you'll be positively encouraging fish away from your hookbait.

I can think of one such feature where I observed fish going through exactly the same path in a wall of reeds. From a great vantage point I could see the fish moving between two reed stems time and time again. It was clearly a historic patrol route and it was obvious where my bait needed to be. The runs that quickly followed were simply the result of following the obvious clues.

PVA

If you asked ten carp anglers to name something that had dramatically changed the face of carp fishing, I dare say most would pick the hair rig or boilies as the biggest of the big. If I asked the same question, I'd say PVA.

Poly vinyl acetate (PVA) is a product of the chemical industry, and has had a huge impact on carp fishing in recent years. It's led directly to the capture of thousands of carp, and I'd go so far as to say that without it an awful lot of carp would simply not have been caught, because it arms the average angler with the means to catch fish no matter what the type of venue. In simple terms, PVA has been a great leveller.

Its principle feature is that it's quite strong when dry but quickly dissolves on contact with water. As long as you buy decent quality PVA it'll literally dissolve to nothing. It's also a versatile product. You can buy solid tape, string and bags that look like they're made of plastic film, or you can get fine mesh that's been spun into tubes inside which you can trap free offerings and tie off to form a sealed bag.

In this chapter I'll look at the different types of PVA and show you how and when to use them.

How to tie a stringer

The oldest type of PVA product is string, or tape, and although it's fallen out of favour in recent times the presentation it produces is still very productive, and catches carp. This sequence shows you how to tie a PVA 'stringer'.

1 You need some PVA tape, such as the Nash, Kryston, Korda or Avid products (personally I prefer tape to string, as it grips the baits better). Cut off 12in.

2 Get a stringer needle (basically just a long baiting needle) and thread the number of boilies you want to feed

on to it. Place the needle on the tape and slide the boilies from needle to PVA to create the 'string'.

3 Tie one end of the tape to the hook, turn it and tie the opposite end.

4 The finished rig exposes the tape so that water can attack and melt it quickly.

5 In the water the PVA dissolves and the hookbait is left lying next to the freebies within a matter of minutes.

How to tie a PVA bag

This is made using fine filaments of PVA thread that are spun into a fine mesh. However, different manufacturers' mesh bags do slightly different things: some feature a fine mesh for carrying small baits, while others have their diameter narrowed to produce aerodynamic bags for long-range casting.

Fox, Nash, 30-Plus and Kryston all produce fine PVA mesh, but I tend to stick by three that have never let me down and are very easy to work with. These are produced by Avid, E-S-P and Korda. In all truth I don't think it makes a huge difference which of them you use.

One final point. PVA bags are one of the very best ways to avoid tangles, because the added weight and resistance provided by the bag spreads the hooklink out in flight, and keeps the hookbait separated from the leger. If you've had problems with tangles, the PVA bag could be your solution.

1 I use two versions of PVA mesh in two different diameters. I use what Korda call their Long Chuck PVA mesh, and the size up from it, the Boilie version. I also use similar diameters of Avid's mesh.

2 To tie up a bag, start by loading the PVA tube with bait. I tend to use a palm-full of pellets or two or three boilies that I break up into 'boilie crumb'. This releases more of the bait's smell.

4 Twist the mesh several times to tighten the threads around the bait and grip them tightly. (Tight PVA bags burst open more violently and spread bait further.) With the PVA bowstring tight around the bait, pinch the twisted section of PVA to stop it unravelling and throw a single overhand loop in the mesh above the bag of bait and

3 Shake the tube to ensure all the bait is at the bottom, then allow some of the PVA to slide off the tube.

close the knot. Tie another knot just above the first one and cut the PVA between the two knots. This releases a tight bag that casts well and will burst open quickly. The knot at the end of the PVA is ready for the next bag.

5 Prepare your bait on the 'hair'.

6 Complete with a boilie stop.

7 Put the baited hook through several strands of PVA. You could cast out like this, and many people do, but I prefer to fix it more securely to withstand casting and sinking through the water to reach the deck.

8 Twist the strands of PVA that the hook is slid under to tighten strands around the hook.

9 Slide the hook point under several more strands of PVA to securely fasten the bag. Never hook the knot – it takes ages to dissolve.

10 Put one dissolving foam nugget on the hook.

11 Then lick a second piece and sandwich it around the hook shank, trapping the hook between the two pieces of foam.

12 Pinch the foam at both ends. Because it's been wetted the foam goes slightly sticky, and this allows both nuggets to be pinched together. This completes the finished rig, which is ready for casting.

13 Once cast out the PVA mesh splits open and the baits are flung out of the bag alongside the hookbait. It's as tight a baiting patch as it's possible to achieve, and is the ultimate way to advertise your hookbait.

14 This shows a variation on the boilie theme, this time using pellets in the bag instead. Pellets can't be fed very far, so the ability to cast 80–100 yards and lay down a tiny patch of pellets offers you something very different.

How to tie a PVA stick

This set-up is essentially just a slightly different way of tying a PVA bag. Personally I'm not a fan of using big bags, and use little ones that deliver a snack of bait instead.

1 First ensure the hooklink is attached to the lead set-up with a quick-change system. I use Korda's Ring Klip and Link Loop, which allows the hooklink to be taken off and reapplied in seconds.

2 Use the narrowest Long Chunk PVA mesh and fill it with groundbait or very finely crushed boilies that won't mask the hook. I like to use the Korda Krusher to make fine crumbs.

3 Load the tube.

4 Use the compressing stick to pack it down tightly. Then, as before, let the PVA slide off the tube. Now you can see why it's called a 'stick'.

5 Follow the same procedure as before to produce a tight bag packed with bait. Then thread it on a long stringer needle on to which you've already slid a short length of silicon tubing.

6 Hook the hooklink on to the needle and pull back through the stick.

7 Sink the hook into the base of the bag and clip it on to the lead system.

8 Slide the silicon tubing up over the clip and you're ready to cast out.

How to make a perfect PVA parcel

Soluble bags are made using a film of PVA, which is fused together to form an envelope that's perfect for holding baits and even attractors. But to use such bags effectively you've got to tie up a very specific rig that's been purpose-designed to cope with being packed within the confines of a bag. So before I show you how to tie a bag let's look first at the rig with which you'll use it.

Tying a PVA bag rig

The key thing to note about tying a rig to go inside a small bag is that you have to make the hooklink around 4in long. A longer hooklink of 8–12in will lead to the hook length being coiled around the inside of the bag, which is a recipe for tangles and poor bite registration, as a fish could pick up the hookbait without pricking itself against the weight of the leger. The bait could then be spat out, leaving you oblivious to the fact that a fish has closed in on your bait.

It's also essential to make the leger an especially safe set-

up. Because the rig is an inline set-up where it runs along the mainline it would be easy to accept the leger couldn't be ejected when a fish is hooked. That way you put up with a sub-standard rig. But this is a crazy choice to make and will cost you fish in the net.

One of the very best situations in which to use a PVA bag is where the weed in a lake is particularly bad and you want to use a presentation that ensures the hooklink and hookbait reach the lake bed in an untangled state.

A PVA bag does this job superbly, so it's essential the rig is able to drop the leger when a fish is hooked. As I said earlier, a rig that can't drop the lead is one that almost guarantees you'll lose fish, as the weed will wrap around the leger and snag the hooked fish.

There are two solutions to this, based on the same principle – ie ensuring that the swivel or plug is pulled out of the lead recess, allowing the lead to fall out of the tail rubber. (The graphic on page 63 illustrates what I mean.)

Solution one

1 First thread some anti-tangle tubing on to the mainline, followed by a Korda tail rubber on to the tubing. I'd suggest not going any lighter than 15lb for the mainline if weed is present. Then tie the mainline to the same end of the swivel as the hooklength is already tied. A ring swivel is good for this, as it allows more movement.

2 Push the loose end of the swivel into the lead, then lay the tubing alongside the lead and push the tail rubber on to the other end.

Solution two

This is essentially the same but uses components specifically designed for inline drop-off systems.

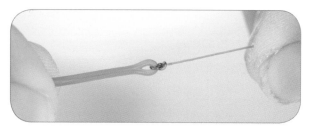

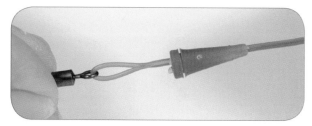

1 First tie a bare Korda Safe Zone leader to 15lb nylon mainline. In weedy water I wouldn't risk going any lighter.

2 Thread the tail rubber at the top of the drop-off leger down the leader. This gadget is designed to dump the lead when a fish is hooked.

3 Clip the insert to the leader ring and then clip on your hooklength.

4 Cover the hooklength clip with 2cm of silicone tubing.

5 Push the Avid inset into the base of the leger, line the leader up in the groove and then push on the tail rubber.

6 In the event of a take and the fish piling into weed the leger pulls out of the tail rubber and stem and is quickly dropped.

Making a PVA bag

Bags can be made freehand, but this simply makes the job extra-fiddly and wastes time. The Fox Rapide Load and Avid Bag Loader are two almost identical gadgets that make bag-tying both quick and easy. I describe the subtle differences between them below, so that you can make up your own mind regarding which you use. Personally I rate them both very highly and use them equally without giving a moment's thought to it. The simple fact is that they both make PVA bag fishing easy.

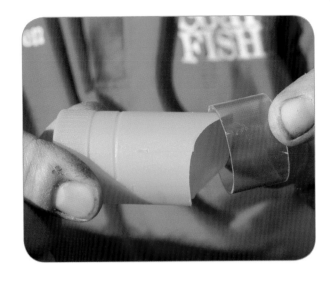

1 The Fox Rapide Load has a piece of flat plastic that's curved into a funnel.

2 Squeeze the plastic and fit the supplied ring to fix the funnel shape.

3 Slip the bag over the funnel and release the ring so the plastic expands.

4 The plastic sheet has tiny teeth around the end which grip the PVA bag.

5 Drop the rig into the bag and pull the leader into the slot to grip it. Fill roughly a third of the bag with your chosen bait so that the hookbait is buried in the bottom of the bag.

6 Now release the leger and position it on top of the bait. Add bait until the leger stem is almost covered.

7 Now comes the clever bit! Lick around the edge of the PVA bag dampening it rather than soaking it.

9 As the PVA almost pulls off the loader, push the bag through the centre of it. This folds over the damp rim of PVA and sticks the bag down on itself. The plastic loader springs open to release the finished bag.

10 To finish the bag the corners are pulled out, licked and stuck down.

8 Slowly twist the bag, a process that closes the bag and pulls the PVA off the loader.

11 The finished bag ready to be cast out. It'll quickly melt and release the bait.

Avid's similar inline bag system differs only slightly, and which you choose is up to you. As I've said, both kits are excellent and will catch more than their share of carp. The loading stage is essentially the same:

1 Bag goes on the loader.

2 Rig goes in position.

3 Bait is added.

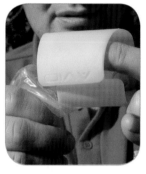

4 Rig ends up sitting in the top layer.

5 The bag is then twisted to close it and pull it off the loader, releasing the little plastic sheet and the rig from each other.

6 Pinch the top of the bag to stop it unravelling. PVA tape is wrapped around the twist and it's tied off with PVA tape.

7 The top of the bag is trimmed.

8 Then the ends are pulled out, dampened and stuck down to tighten the bag.

9 The finished bag boasts a bullet shape that casts for miles, especially if you ignore the largest sizes of bag and just use the smallest ones.

Because of the way it's made there isn't a double layer of PVA at the top of the Avid bag to slow its dissolving rate, and it melts quickly and evenly. But as I've said, overall there's little difference, and I rate both systems highly.

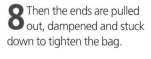

GETTING A RUN

This is it – the moment of truth. You've picked a swim, baited it and set your trap. The waiting game has ticked by and finally the fish you've set your heart on catching has wandered within your grasp. As the bite alarm signals its arrival the game moves into wholly new territory. You've got your run, and now the job in hand is to bring your fish to the bank, where you can finally cast your eyes upon a carp.

Be it a small one, a big one, or a giant that revises your imagination about just how big a fish can grow, doesn't really matter. It's the thrill of the chase, the elation of the run, that will spark off a memorable moment of excitement and achievement.

In this chapter we look at what happens when a fish picks up your hookbait, how you bring it safely to the bank and, even more importantly, how you return it to the water none the worse for its experience.

When a stunning fish like this common picks up your bait, it's important not to panic. Just stay calm and get it right.

The thrill of the run

When your bite alarm indicates a fish has picked up your bait you react instantly, first with a pulse rate that rockets skywards and second with a series of movements that in time will come naturally and smoothly without the slightest hesitation.

It's these movements I'm going to look at first – how do you strike into a run, what's the best way to play a fish, and how do you land it? Because when the bite alarm goes you've got to be drilled on what to do next. Get your next steps right and disaster should be averted.

The run

When a carp stumbles into your trap, sucks up your hookbait and feels the resistance of your leger as the hook takes hold in its mouth, you should be rewarded with a golden moment – a screaming run that lights up your bite alarm and sends an ear-splitting shriek battering at your lugholes.

That split-second is what you go carp fishing for. The sight and sound of a carp run is one of the most thrilling things in carp fishing, especially on new waters or lakes where you've set your heart on the capture of a particular carp. But this thrilling moment can quickly become the source of heartbreak. If the line falls slack or breaks with a shuddering *crack* the thought of impending glory quickly turns to despair.

In some cases there's nothing you can do about it. A metal hook is a tiny piece of hardware upon which your success or failure hangs, and there are times when nothing you did can be blamed for your failure to convert fish on the hook to fish on the bank.

But the fact is, sometimes your actions have a fundamental impact on whether you succeed or fail, and it's always baffled me why so little attention is paid to successfully landing the fish you hook. An inability to stack the odds in your favour now can undo an awful lot of patient work that's gone before. Safely landing carp isn't a lottery.

When your bite alarm screams and the indicator either drops to the floor as a fish moves towards you, or slams into the rod as line is pulled off the reel, you're called to action. What you do next has a huge impact on whether the fish ends up having its picture taken or swims away scot-free:

1 When you get a run you mustn't panic and strike violently. That's just liable to yank the hook out rather than pull it in. The vast majority of carp rigs are self-hooking rigs to some extent all you need is a smooth, steady pressure to pull the hook home.

2 Disengage the bait runner system if you're using one, or tighten the drag if you're not. Keeping the rod held vertically let the pressure build until there is a hefty bend in the rod and line slowly starts to click off the reel.

3 Now this period of the fight is likely to see the fish wanting to put as much distance as possible between it and you. Don't panic. Unless there are snags in the vicinity let it do so and let line tick off the reel. A running carp is a fish using up its energy.

4 Look out for snags, weed beds or any obstruction that could spell disaster. Follow the line entering the water and look up to see where the fish is heading, if disaster looms tighten the drag and apply more pressure or side strain to stop the fish.

5 After a short while the run will slow down and will eventually stop, with the fish just tugging on the end of the line. This is the moment where you take control – or at least you should do – as you get the chance to take the fight to the fish.

6 You should have your free hand tweak the drag system to control the resistance applied to the fish pulling off line. It is far, far better to control a fish through the drag system rather than by manically back winding line off the reel. Carp often make a bolt for freedom and can do so with tremendous speed and power, the drag system responds instantly which you simply can't do if you are back-winding to release line off the reel. This gives you far more control.

7 With the rod held almost upright you should be able to feel whether a fish is running or not and when you feel the power wane take that as your cue to gain line. Adopt a routine of pump and wind – lower the rod to gain line then ease the rod back. This enables you to wind line onto the reel. Bit by bit you'll draw the fish nearer to the net. Just be aware that at any moment a carp can wrench control again. This is where the drag system kicks in to release line and avoid breakage.

8 Depending on whether the fish is tiring now's the time to think about readying the net. As ever make sure the drag system is fine-tuned to release line as soon as a hooked fish demands and position the net directly in front of you.

9 Never be in a rush to get a carp in the net. Take your time and allow the fish to have line if that's what it really wants to do. Some anglers see releasing line as an admission of defeat, it isn't it simply means you're tuned into the fish and less likely to pull the hook.

10 Now it's crunch time. As the fish's runs get shorter and the carp comes closer to your bank and the surface it's easy to rush things – be patient. Carp are lost by a lack of patience rather than anything else, take your time and be prepared to release line.

11 If the fish is ready for netting don't pull it onto the surface too soon. The pressure on the hook hold is much greater when the fish is on the surface so let the carp stay below the surface and turn it back and forth to ease it in. When the carp is running out of fight it's time for the dangerous bit, ease the fish onto the surface and push forward with the net. Be aware the carp may summon up a last gasp dive at this point. The drag should be adjusted to release line and avoid disaster.

12 Sink the net, ease the fish towards and over the net cord. Don't be in a rush to lift the net, wait until the carp's nose nuts the spreader block before lift the cord and wrap the mesh around the fighting fish. Job done! The fish is in the net, you can relax and check you are organised for the weighing and photographing procedure, this avoids unnecessary stress on the fish later. Leave the fish in the water until you are ready.

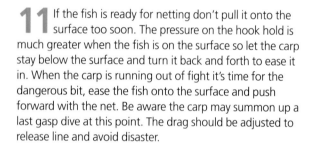

Out of the water...then back again

Now comes the key risk period for the carp: bringing it out of the water.

Carp are strong, hard-fighting fish, but they're still vulnerable to poor handling and sloppy fish care, so you must pay close attention to what you're doing. Stressing just how important it is that you're well organised might sound a bit boring, but believe me, this isn't a process to be side-stepped. The carp's welfare is at stake and you MUST take it very seriously.

The sequence I've put together here details how to look after the fish you catch so that no harm comes to them and they go back in just the same condition as they were when you hooked them.

Follow this guide and you'll successfully unhook, weigh, photograph and release your fish.

1 This is my unhooking station, with a Nash Carp Cradle taking centre stage. This is a fabulous unhooking mat that's thoroughly padded and also sports a flap that can be closed over a fish to stop it jumping clear of the mat.

2 The mat is clipped to the metal frame so that the fish is supported off the ground. No matter how much the fish bounces around it can't damage itself and lies in a padded enclosure. Note the weigh sling positioned in the base of the unhooking mat.

3 Zero the scales before locating the weigh sling on the unhooking system.

4 By the side of the mat should be a small pouch holding your all-important fish-care products. You should have skin repair lotions to smear into any hook marks or into any sores on the fish's body, plus a bucket or bowl of water. Nash and Korda make excellent carp care products.

5 Unship the net arms from the landing net handle, roll down the mesh – making sure the fish's fins are flattened against its sides – and carry it to the unhooking mat. Lay the fish on the mat, which should be thoroughly soaked first.

6 Unhook the carp by prizing the metal out of it using forceps or your finger, being careful to avoid hooking yourself. Personally I use my fingers, as I can feel the exact amount of pressure being placed on the fish and can tease the hook out.

7 Place the hook in the butt ring of your rod, tighten up the line and lay the rod out of harm's way.

8 Lift up the fish's head and then its tail so that you can remove the landing net and leave the fish in the sling.

9 Run the hook on the base of the scales through the two loops fitted to the straps on the weigh sling. The sling should be wetted and zeroed on the scales before you land a fish. With the fish retained in the sling, lift the scales and record the weight.

10 Lower the fish back on to the mat and detach the scales. Wet the fish with the pot of water stationed to hand by the side of the mat. Not only is a wet and gleaming fish nicer to photograph but it's also healthier for the carp.

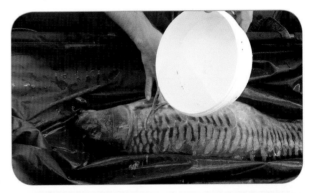

11 With photographer in position directly in front of the fish and ready to fire off pictures, slide your hands under the carp. One hand goes around the wrist of its tail, the other gains a firm handle around its pectoral fins.

12 Grip the fish firmly. Carp are more likely to be damaged by being held too limply than too tight – the fish can too easily jump out of a weak grip and damage itself. Hold the carp firmly and lift it for the camera.

13 Hold the carp out and make sure it's held directly over the mat so that if it flaps it can simply be laid down on the mat to stop any harm coming to it. If the fish is fighting and flapping don't rush it – lay it on the mat and keep it wet.

14 Here's the perfect way to hold a carp – tightly held, low to the ground, over the mat, and the photographer has cropped in tightly to show off the fish to its best. What a cracking carp this is thanks to the way it's being cared for.

15 With pictures taken, lay the carp in the sling, check for any sores and treat them.

16 Gather together the two sides of the sling and carry the fish to the water. I use Nash's Weightlifter sling, as the fabric is very tough and the metal poles are very strong.

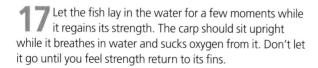

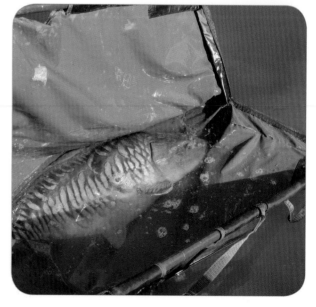

17 Let the fish lay in the water for a few moments while it regains its strength. The carp should sit upright while it breathes in water and sucks oxygen from it. Don't let it go until you feel strength return to its fins.

As you stand and watch your capture slowly return to its home, pause and treasure the moment. Then do what we all do – go back and review the pictures; they're your memories for the future.

My trusted work colleague, top photographer and fishing friend Mick can catch them as well as take the pictures.

Long-time fishing friend Brian Skoyles with a big smile and a lovely French mirror.

They don't come any better than this lovely linear.

FLOATER FISHING

Watching a carp feeding on the surface, noisily slurping in baits as it moves ever nearer to your hookbait, is one of the most thrilling ways to catch fish. When that carp finally sucks in your floating bait and you connect with the culprit chaos breaks out as it powers away and line tears off your reel. It's awesome stuff, and the thrill of hooking fish on the surface is something to treasure.

Too few anglers seriously floater fish, by which I mean few actually go fishing with that intention in the forefront of their mind rather than merely as a secondary tactic when the leger rods don't produce.

In this chapter I'll detail the kit you need, show you how to tie an effective rig, how feeding pays a central role in getting takes and then how you land your fish.

The magic of seeing a carp slurp your bait down is something special.

Kit essentials

When you're trying to catch carp off the top you need to fine down your kit but still keep it all balanced. What I mean by this is that there's no point using 6lb hook links in a weedy jungle, as you'll simply lose everything you hook. Similarly, there's little point scaling-down hooks and line only to fish them on a 3.5lb long-range casting tool. The rod is simply too powerful for the kit you're using and there's almost no chance of you actually landing anything you hook.

For 99% of the floater fishing I do I use the Fox Floater rod. I'll stress again that I'm not sponsored to give this

recommendation – I simply l-o-v-e this rod for floater fishing. It's 12ft long, has a through action and a test curve of 2¼lb. This means it's strong yet beautifully forgiving and bends right into the butt. When you hook a carp you can be sure the rod has a lightning action to set the hook, yet will bend beautifully to prevent the hook hold failing or the line breaking. I've fished in super-weedy venues and caught 30lb-plus carp with relatively little problem using this rod. (If you're getting the feeling that I love using it you're not even halfway there!)

I really like the smoothness of the clutch on this Daiwa Whisker 2600.

For the reel to team up with it, again I keep it relatively small to balance with the rod, and use a Daiwa Whisker 2600. This is loaded with 10lb or 12lb Berkley Sensation line, the former for clearer swims while the latter is reserved for weedy venues. In really clear venues with no snags I'll occasionally drop down to 8lb line if the fish are particularly line-shy.

As for hooklinks, well, I've got to thank my great friend Brian Skoyles for putting me on to this one, called Stroft GTM. It's exceptionally thin for its breaking strain and is wonderfully limp.

Brian is without doubt one of the best floater anglers I've ever fished with, and has worked at his approach, so that when he told me this was *the* line to get I did as I was told! It's thin for its breaking strain and doesn't dictate the progression of the hookbait due to its lack of stiffness. This is especially important when fishing for line-shy fish, as it doesn't make the bait behave suspiciously. I carry a range of breaking strains, 9lb, 11lb and 14lb being the versions I most commonly use.

Stroft GTM is my number-one hooklength line.

The Korda Mixa hook is great for surface fishing – strong, with a wide gape and not too heavy in the wire. The Drennan Super Specialist Barbel is another great hook for surface fishing.

As for hooks, I now use the Korda Mixa hook in sizes 10 and 12, designed for floater fishing. I've found them to be exceptionally reliable and good for getting bites very quickly. I also carry Drennan's Super Specialist Barbel, which is a lighter wire model that's incredibly strong and sharp.

When deciding on floats, I've settled on just two types, both made by Korda, which cover all the fishing situations I seem to encounter. Their Kruiser is a float that sits upright in the water with the line passing through the tip of the float. The rest of it is buried beneath the surface so that the wind can't catch hold of it and drag it (and therefore the hookbait) unnaturally through the water. I use this float when I want to cast into a fairly tight area and keep the rig there for the maximum amount of time.

The other model I use, the Interceptor, is designed to do exactly the opposite! In this case the line runs through the entire length of the float, which then lies horizontally on the surface when it's cast out. With the float lying flat on the surface, it's designed to be very stable and help move the hookbait naturally. To wised-up carp the natural movement of baits on the surface is hugely important. I've watched fish inspect and refuse baits that just look a bit wrong. On the other hand I've seen them race in for a bait that's behaving as if it was a free offering.

Getting your rig to behave properly is one of the keys to succeeding on the surface.

The two Korda controllers will cover most situations.

The Korda Interceptor lies flat on the surface.

THE TWO MAIN CONTROLLER OPTIONS

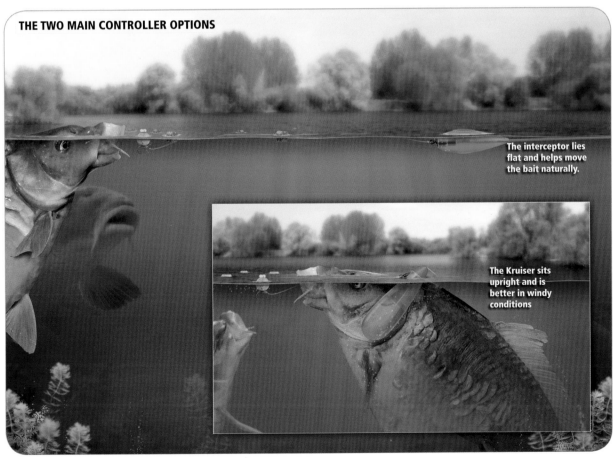

The interceptor lies flat and helps move the bait naturally.

The Kruiser sits upright and is better in windy conditions

Surface baits

There are lots of bait floats, but I've got a few favourites that I habitually stick by.

First up is the common or garden dog mixer biscuit. Literally millions of these little biscuits have been thrown at carp over the years, and they're still very successful. They can be used straight from the bag, although I prefer to soak and flavour them. Pour 100ml of water in a bottle, add 5ml of flavour (Nutrabaits Wonderfruit and Tutti Frutti are two favourites) and 2ml of Sweet Cajouser, then slop it on the biscuits. Put a lid on the bucket holding the mixers and the liquid and shake them until all the liquid is sucked up. Turn the bucket every ten minutes or so until all the biscuits aren't sticking together.

As long as they're left two or three hours the rock hard biccies will soften right the way through and you can mount them on a hair rig. I try to prepare mine the evening before a floater fishing trip, as they soften then harden again as they dry out slightly. Of course, this isn't always possible, so my freezer always has a carrier bag of 'emergency mixers' in it that are flavoured and softened then frozen. They thaw in no time.

In the summer I often scale up the tub size and flavour in bulk so I have several bags in the freezer.

I often add a dusting of dye before flavouring the mixers. When the water and flavour is added the dye is

Oiling up

1 My present surface bait … Hinders Floating Pellets.

2 I like to oil and flavour them.

3 Pour 200ml of your chosen oil (in this case sunflower oil) into a spare bottle.

4 I have a spare bottle marked up so that I don't have to measure it out each time.

activated and the floaters take on the colour. It's a moot point as to whether the carp can actually tell the difference or not, but I feel better about using coloured mixers rather than plain ones.

But I have to say that dog food isn't as good as it used to be. I don't think the biscuits are as buoyant, and they tend to be more erratically shaped, so they don't catapult as well. I don't suppose we can complain, mind you, as they're being made for dogs to eat after all, and there's very little reason to make them aerodynamic!

I've therefore started to use Hinders floating pellets more often, and they're better. They come in consistent sizes and they have a much more fishy smell to them. I enhance this by 'oiling them up'. This is very easy to do, as the picture sequence will show. I just make an oil mix of 200ml of oil flavoured with 20ml of the awesome Blue Oyster flavouring. It might not sound a lot, but since I was put on to flavouring these baits by Brian Skoyles I've noticed just how avidly the fish suck them down.

These baits make up the vast majority of my fishing, but I do carry Sonubaits' floating pellets and have found them very good too, again with just a sheen of extra oil added to them.

From time to time I even still catch on good old-fashioned bread crust. I dare say most anglers would scoff at such an old tactic, but the fact that it's old makes it all the more interesting in my book, as lots of fish will have forgotten or never seen it. Once bread is soggy it's very easy to strike through, and I also like the texture of it, as do the fish. It's not a bait I base my floater fishing on but it's one I often carry.

I also always have some Sonubaits floating pellets with me. A great alternative.

Bread crust will still catch you carp in the right circumstances.

5 Add your flavour, in this case 20ml of Nutrabaits Blue Oyster.

7 Put your pellets into a bucket and drizzle a small amount of oil over them. Shake thoroughly.

6 Shake thoroughly.

8 Repeat until all the pellets have a slight sheen to them.

9 The final result ready to go, pellets with that bit extra!

Making a floater rig

The sequence coming up shows you how to tie a very basic rig for floater fishing with the upright Korda Kruiser float. The upright controller is designed to catch fish feeding in a tight area where you want to minimise or slow down drifting.

But first we need a way of attaching the floater to the hook. My favourite method is using a reverse hair. It's difficult to tie but it's worth making the effort, as it helps the carp hook itself as it takes the floater.

Tying the reverse hair

1 You'll need your hook, a bait band and some fine braid.

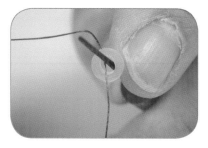

2 Get some of the finest braid you can. I use 20lb Daiwa Tournament Braid. Cut off a foot or so then thread a very small bait band on it.

3 Tie a very small loop in the braid, trapping the band.

4 Place a needle behind the knot and tighten up to this rather than the band itself.

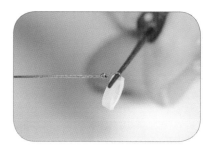

5 Because the braid isn't tight around the band it can still move slightly. This helps you get movement in the bait and aids the final presentation.

6 Trim off the spare braid.

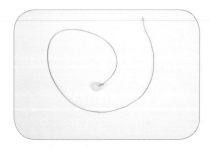

7 Your hair braid complete with bait band is now ready to whip to the shank of the hook, so the band is next to the hook eye.

8 Now the tricky bit! Start by laying the band near the hook eye and form a loop in the braid lying along the hook.

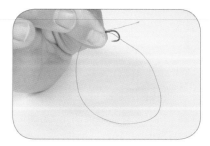

9 Position the end of the braid poking just beyond the length of the hook. It's important where you place the braid.

10 Pinch the loop, wrap it over the hook and round the tag end of the line.

11 Whip back down the shank towards the eye ten times. The braid is now whipped down the shank.

12 Holding the loop, pull the end of the tag. You may need to wet the braid with saliva to help the line slide.

13 The knot will bite below the hook eye with the band positioned just above the whipping.

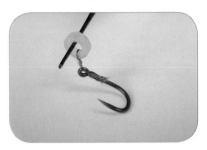

14 Push it up to touch the eye of the hook and twist it so that the band is on the back of the eye. Trim off the tag of braid to produce the finished reverse hair. This brings the hookbait on to the back of the hook.

Once your reverse hair is tied the hooklength itself is very simple. Just tie the hook to your hooklength line (I use a Palomar knot for this) and secure a swivel at the other end, again with a Palomar knot. I like to make my hooklength as long as possible without making casting too difficult. About 6ft is a good compromise. And now you have your hooklength and your controller.

Tying the rig

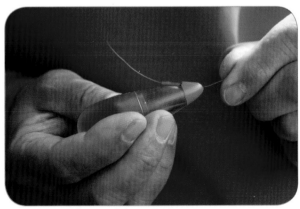

1 Run the float down the mainline. I tend to use 8–12lb line.

2 Use a five-turn grinner knot to attach the hooklink to the line.

3 Slide the float down to the swivel on the hooklink and push the float's silicon sleeve over the swivel to semi-fix the hooklink to the float.

4 The finished rig is easy to tie and use. Just bait it and cast out!

Using a floater rig

Now we'll move on to how you put a floater rig to use, courtesy of surface fanatic Brian:

There's no doubt that if you get it right this can be one of the most dramatic and successful tactics of the summer months, and I still can't believe it's so underused. A lot of anglers only turn to the surface when all else has failed, and I personally find this bizarre.

Floater fishing should be seen as just as good a method as any other, and if you pick your time to use it then there should be no doubting its effectiveness. It's certainly not a second-best tactic that only comes good when the sun shines. True, it might be a waste of time in winter, but from spring through to autumn it can be a great method that offers you that little bit extra just when you often need it.

Anyway, let's look at the tactics of getting fish feeding on the surface. We went to a lovely water called Lakeside near Pocklington, East Yorkshire. It's not renowned for big fish, but it's immaculately run, and the carp stocks are high, mostly high singles and doubles – and they love a floater. Where better to do a picture sequence?

1 The first thing you've got to do is find your fish. Don some polarised sunglasses, or if you're a specs-wearer like me, get yourself some prescription polarised glasses. They cut through the surface glare and make spotting cruising fish so much easier.

2 Walk around the lake looking for signs of fish up in the water or near the surface. Most obviously look for shadows or fish cruising just below the surface, but also look for swirls or eruptions on the surface. Carp often spook each other when they're on the top.

3 Once you've found some fish set up nearby. Ideally look for the wind coming from directly behind you or across your shoulders, so that your controller float isn't blown straight back in towards the bank.

4 Don't cast out. This might seem crazy, but in most circumstances it doesn't pay to cast at fish you've just found on the surface. Instead, start to loose feed floaters, drifting them across the surface.

5 Keep watching for fish swirling on the surface or cruising below the surface. Particularly watch for signs of fish actively competing for floaters on the top. Once carp are racing each other you're well on your way.

6 Only when you've seen the carp confidently slurp down floaters with wild abandon is it time to get your rod out and make a cast.

7 Make sure you overcast the area you've been feeding and slowly draw the hookbait back towards the bait. When the float is cast out, slowly draw it back to the feeding fish, but don't pull it right into feeding activity. Let the float lie on the outskirts of the loose fed area and wait for the fish to come towards the rig.

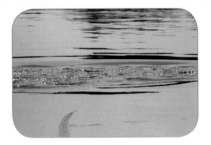

8 The hookbait should lie on the surface, and will drift along on the top. This is the point where you can expect to get takes, although there's no reason why you should strike – the controller is like a floating leger and hooks the fish for you. As the fish swirls on your hook bait, be patient, watch the controller. When the fish is hooked you'll see an ever-increasing explosion of water and the line will start to zip across the surface. Don't panic or overreact – just lift the rod and let the reel's clutch take over … Magic!

9 Presuming that you hook the fish, you'll need to play it carefully, but not too softly – if you've got the balance right the rod shouldn't overpower the line and hook combo, and you'll eventually have the fish ready for netting.

10 If all goes well, the carp should be brought slowly towards the net and into the mesh. This is why having the balance of your gear right is so important. Fish will still fight hard, but the softness of the rod compensates for its lack of power.

11 Here's the payoff for a couple of hours' careful floater fishing – a brace of hard-fighting carp that took the hookbait and hooked themselves against the weight of the controller float. Get it right and floater fishing can be relaxing, exciting and very productive.

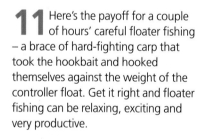

That moment when time stands still, as a confidently feeding carp approaches your perfectly presented hookbait and you just *know* it's going to 'have' it. Go on – going, going ... *gone*!

Changing the situation

Of course, carp can and do change the 'rules' of floater fishing on you at any time. Look out for situations where the fish have learned to back-off from baited areas and spots that are loose-fed with freebies. Streetwise fish often take one or two floaters then drift away. If this is the case a pre-emptive cast can pay off, where you put out your hookbait before you've fed anything at all. If the fish have learned to take the first floaters to hit the surface, make sure your hookbait is one of them.

I've also come across waters where the fish rarely take a floater through the day but take them last thing before night, when they can't see the line very well. It's safe to suspect that this is the behaviour of seriously cute fish. They're so good at spotting the odd one out that you've got to make it harder for them to spot your rig by using finer tackle. You've also got to be in the right place at the right time for that short period when they're easier to catch.

Finally there are fish that are stalked on floaters. These are singular fish that are often found sheltering in beds of lilies, holes in the weed or under a bush. A single floater, flicked into the hole, is usually the perfect way to tempt a carp. These are fish often stalked in the edge rather than being caught out of open water.

This is a situation you often encounter late in the evening, when fish have crept into the margins and are mopping up what's been left behind. I once filmed a sequence for the Discovery channel where I fished for a carp that was sucking grubs and bugs from within the 'scum line' of collected rubbish and fluff blown on to the surface. It was a tremendous sequence where I crept silently in, lowered my floater into the scum and then watched a pair of lips break through the surface and suck in my hookbait. The fight that followed was true 'seat of the pants'-type fishing, and hugely enjoyable.

That sums up the magic of floater fishing – it can be full-on fighting in a split second.

Timing

As a final thought, many anglers are put off short sessions for carping, thinking that if you can't 'bivvy up', stay overnight etc, it's not worth going. But surface fishing is the opposite. It's perfect for the carper tight on time. Often during the heat of the day, carp will be in the upper layers just drifting about on the surface, but they are just taking the sun, and not too keen to feed. As evening arrives, the temperature drops a little, any breeze fades away and the carp 'think food'. Now can be the best time to catch carp off the top. I can think of no better way to relax and unwind after a hard day's work, and I know of many surface fishing fanatics that will totally agree!

Surface fanatic Graham Drewery loves nothing better than a couple of hours' surface fishing in the evening after a hard day's work.

STALKING

Stalking has come into fashion in recent years as more anglers have realised that creeping around in the undergrowth can pay big dividends, and they're setting traps in the margins that can fool the biggest and wariest of fish. Personally I realised what I was missing about five years ago, when I started to fish a lake that was heavily wooded and full of marginal snags and weed beds that you knew could hold carp.

I realised from my very first trip to the lake that I had to forget my normal preconceptions if I wanted to catch carp during the short trips I had at my disposal. The fish in this lake spend a huge amount of time creeping around the edge. Like ghosts in the night, they creep around the edge tucking themselves into weed channels and under overhanging trees. It's the sort of venue that really hones my carp-fishing senses and focuses my attention on the tiniest of spots.

It's fascinating, invigorating carping, and I can honestly say that in the last few years I've enjoyed my fishing more than ever, despite the fact that a young family has meant I've never had so little free time to actually go! What's more, I'm not alone – a huge number of carpers are facing the same balancing act, where they want to go carping but simply can't balance the demands of work and family long enough to free-up time to fish.

If time is an issue for you then this chapter is full of information that'll help you catch fish very efficiently when time is tight. Even if time isn't so much of an issue, I still think you should read this chapter and ask yourself one simple question: am I missing out on something?

If you suspect the answer to the question is 'yes', then the next few pages will provide a great launch pad to a new and exciting part of your carp life. Until now you might have only gone stalking as a last resort. I'm hoping to convince you it can be one of the best ways to succeed.

The kit you need

First I'm going to look at the tackle that's needed for catching fish in the edges, because it is different to what you need for fishing at longer range. In fact I'll actually go so far as to say that in many cases you simply can't use kit that's made for legering at longer ranges – you've got to use specialist kit that's far more suited to close-quarters angling.

The first thing to realise is that short rods are essential. Rather than simply using my standard 12ft, 3lb test curve rods I use purpose-made stalking rods between 6ft and 9ft. These dinky rods are used because nine times out of ten you'll be fishing in exceptionally tight areas where there's thick weed, a blanket of vegetation or a mountain of bank-side growth that long rods are simply too cumbersome to cope with.

When I started dabbling with margin stalking I did what the vast majority of anglers do: I made do with what I had and ended up using really long casting rods and giant reels to match. Eventually, when I was getting my tenth birds' nest of line of the day, I realised it was time to change things. My existing kit was great for casting, but useless for dropping a rig close to the bank.

A purpose-made stalking rod is essential, as is a reel with much-reduced capacity. I have a range of stalking tools, from a 9ft E-S-P Stalker rod through to a Greys Prodigy and finally a really short 6ft Fox Twig rod, which is the favourite of ALL my carp rods.

In each case these rods are strong, but they tend to bend right the way through to the butt. Think of them like a short but very strong elastic band and you're on the right lines. This characteristic is vital, because it means they have the power to turn a carp that's bent on reaching a set of marginal snags, yet balance that power with enough suppleness to stop you springing the hooks.

The 6ft Fox Twig rod, which is the favourite of ALL my carp rods.

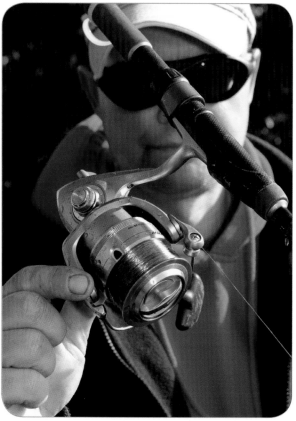

I place my rod on a Fox alarm or Nash Siren – both alert you the moment a fish makes off with your bait, and they also hold the rod very securely.

However, to fully secure the rod I know extra fixing is needed. With the drag screwed down tightly so a fish can't just power off with the rig and find the snags that litter the margins of the best stalking waters, I slip a special fixture over the backrest as a source of extra security.

Made with two cable ties that are interlocked, one of them wraps around the rod while the second is free to be looped over the rear rod rest. When cast out the rod is secured much more tightly by these little additions. That's

The small but powerful Daiwa Emblem 3000-sized reel that's made for swim feeder fishing is ideal for margin stalking.

I would say a 9ft rod and a 6ft one are essential, the longer rod for dealing with slightly more open swims and the shorter one for coping with restrictive spots where trees or bushes stop you using the longer rod.

Next is the reel. Once again I rely on a Daiwa model, but instead of picking my big pit reels I use the small Emblem 3000 size that's made for swim feeder fishing. The main reasons for picking this reel are its lack of size, lower line capacity, strong gearing and slick clutch that can be screwed down tight, either to stop any line being released or to give it only under very heavy stress. When it's loaded with 18lb line so that the line doesn't spring off the spool too readily, you have a set-up that really does perform well when under severe stress.

So, that's the hardware dealt with, and many anglers would settle for that – but my margin stalking has become far more honed than this. For a start I always use thick, strong bank sticks and rod rests that aren't going to fold under the sort of extreme situation that can come with a fast take at close quarters. Fox's great Black Label metal ware is strong and has a wide bore, perfect for securely gripping the bank.

The John Roberts gripper-style rod rest screwed into the rear bank stick grips the rod firmly, and at the front end I place a Fox alarm or Nash Siren. Both alert you the moment a fish makes off with your bait, and they also hold the rod very securely.

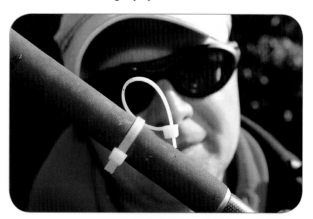

not my idea, by the way, but Martin Locke's of Solar Tackle, so I doff my cap in his direction. A few cable ties from the local 'pound shop' cost next to nothing, but I wouldn't margin fish without them now. Who says carp fishing has to be expensive?

Keep mobile, stay vigilant

Of course, one of the most appealing aspects of margin stalking is the ability to travel light and move in seconds. I regularly fish upwards of six swims in an afternoon. On one memorable day I caught fish from four different swims, and these were good fish too, that weighed over 30lb.

To keep mobile, one of the essentials is to carry the minimum amount of kit. You can't move quickly if you've got to packhorse mountains of kit round the lake. The opening photo of this chapter shows me in my stalking get-up. Now I just need to explain what I'm carrying and why.

The rod

There's no need for a holdall. One or at the most two short rods are carried, and they're permanently baited in case I need to place my hookbait in a hurry!

Polarised glasses

I wear spectacles, so when I'm stalking I use prescription sunglasses to cut out the surface glare – I wouldn't stalk without them.

Polarised glasses are an essential.

Landing net

An E-S-P design that's very strong and has a very long handle that can be used to reach for fish that might be stuck on the other side of a marginal weed bed.

Unhooking mat

A Fox mat that's got high sides to act as a carry all and is heavily padded to protect the fish once it's been landed.

All the gear gets folded up and carried in my high-sided Fox unhooking mat.

Accessories

Inside the mat I have unhooking equipment, weighing kit and a tub carrying plenty of stalking baits.

Legs and motivation!

This might sound daft, but stalking isn't for the lazy. You've got to be prepared to get stung, bitten, cut to ribbons and end up exhausted but exhilarated!

Drab clothing

If you like wearing flaming pink T-shirts, then stick to casting 100 yards! Wear drab clothing and don't move much – it's the movement that gives you away.

Rigging up

Fishing next to snags is real hit-and-hold tactics.

Once you've got the right hardware you need a rig that's strong and won't let you down. Catching carp in the margins can be a testing process, and you don't want kit that simply folds up the moment things get the least bit hairy.

Here's how you tie up the rig I use. It's strong and designed not to fail on you if things do get exciting. It's also a lot heavier than I'd normally use, but this is simply to over-gun for the situation I'm fishing.

I would never, repeat *never, never, never*, advocate anyone to fish for carp in a snaggy maelstrom where the vast majority of hooked fish are lost within seconds of hooking them. It's grossly irresponsible to fish for carp in these situations. You must always fish where the odds are hugely stacked in your favour, and where you're not going to damage any fish you hook.

My reason for using such strong tackle is to make sure I don't leave tackle in a fish if the line brushes a piece of rough ground or a snaggy branch. I'd rather forego runs than fish with kit that's not sufficiently over-gunned to cope with any situation.

Anyway, here's the rig I tie:

If you don't have a good chance of landing the fish safely … don't fish it!

1 I use very strong line and pick 25lb breaking strain E-S-P Two Tone coated braid. It breaks at more than 30lb if tied correctly. Hook-wise, a Korda Wide Gape size 8 or Nash FangX 8 is small enough to bed in but doesn't open up.

2 The hookbait is placed by hand, so I use chunks of bait rather than a round boilie. It pumps out smell and looks less suspicious. As with my other fishing situations, I use Nutrabaits Trigga Ice boilies, with the bait cut down to two 12mm pieces.

3 Tie a small hair on the end of the coated braid.

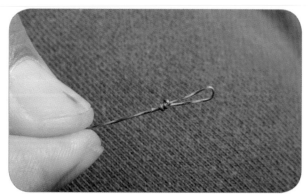

4 Load the two chopped baits on the braid.

5 Thread the line through the back of the hook and position the bait where you want it. Personally I like a big gap between hook and hookbait, as it produces better hook holds.

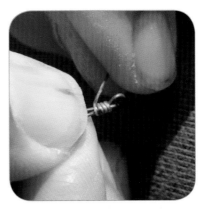

6 Whip down the shank three or four times.

7 Go round the hair and whip down the shank another six times. This is the KD rig that we looked at back in Chapter 4, which produces a great hooking position.

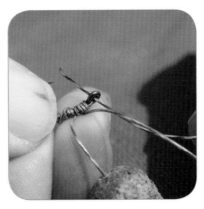

8 Thread the end of the braid back through the rear of the eye.

9 Pull tight so that the hook is fixed on the line.

10 Remove the baits, then use your fingernail or stripper tool to remove 2in of plastic coating so that the hookbait is flexible.

11 Remove a short length of the plastic coating from above the hook as well, so that the hook moves with a high degree of natural flexibility. This isn't a hugely natural-looking rig, so it's essential to maximise the natural movement that does exist.

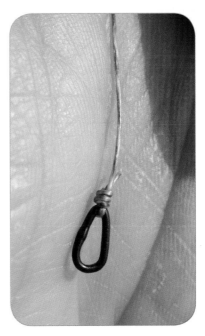

12 Tie a link loop to the other end of a short 6in link.

167

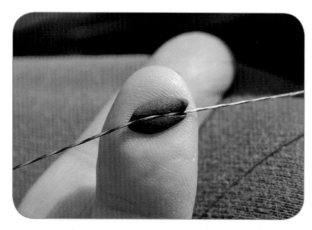

13 Add a small blob of tungsten putty to the line to weigh it down and pin it to the lake bed. Again, this just makes the rig less obvious.

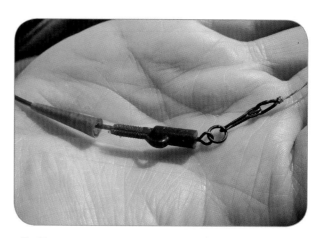

14 Tie a long clay-coloured Korda Safe-Zone leader, complete with lead clip, to the E-S-P 18lb nylon mainline. This is used as a 'rubbing leader' to make the rig resistant to branches or snags that the line may slide against. Slide a 2cm long piece of Korda silicone tubing on to the hooklength, then clip the hooklength on to the lead clip.

15 Slide the 2cm piece of Korda silicone tube back up and over the clip. This is a very secure junction but one that can be swapped in seconds.

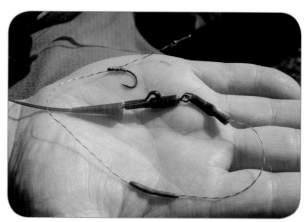

16 The rig is good to go!

17 Add a leger to the leader and note that the clip's tail rubber is only just pushed on. I'm happy to dump the lead as soon as it's done its job and hooked the fish. It makes a carp far less likely to be lost in weedy lakes.

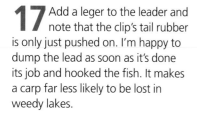

Laying in the rig

When you're margin fishing you're generally laying rigs in likely looking areas or spots where you've actually seen carp ghosting through. In most cases this negates the need for long-range casting and means most baits can either be lowered into the water, placed with an underarm swing or at most placed with a little overarm chuck. The key is placing the hookbait quickly, silently and with the absolute minimum amount of disturbance.

Most of the time it's just a gentle swing to place the hook bait. Just hold the lead and let it swing forward.

At the end of the arc, release the line and let it drop quietly into the water.

In most cases I swing the baited rig gently into the water so that it 'kisses' the water rather than slaps it and then drops to the lake bed. In quite a few swims I can think of I lower it off the rod tip on a tight line and backwind it to the bottom. I can then place the leger and hookbait apart so that the bolt effect is magnified – as soon as a carp picks up the bait it feels the lead and bolts to drag the hook home. That's the theory, anyway. More of that later!

In the right situation I actually place my rig with a special pole cupping kit made by Angling Intelligence (pictured above). Basically this is a pole with a long spoon on the end that the rig and bait is placed in and then shipped out with the bale arm of the reel open so that line peels off. The rig and any free offerings can then be placed on the money. It can also be placed where you can't cast to due to overhanging trees and the like.

This piece of kit could easily be abused by allowing you to place your rig in a snag pit where you stand no chance of landing the fish you hook. However, if you're more responsible this is a great edge to have tucked away in your back pocket.

One of my favourite stalking spots is a very quiet corner of a busy day-ticket fishery. On virtually any spring to autumn day I can go to this lake and catch a carp within an hour (often within ten minutes) on a bait dropped in the margins using the spoon, under a set of overhanging trees. I know that there's no danger to the fish from placing the rig where I do. It's just that a tree overhangs the water and makes casting near to the fish almost impossible; but with the spoon I can get under the branch line and place the rig where only one in twenty casts would land.

In certain situations it's a massive edge that gets you an awful lot more bites. What's more it also allows you to spoon in a porridge of pellet bits, broken boilies and pulverised particles that help cloud the water to disguise the presence of your rig, as well as attract the carp.

Used in the right spot with the right baits I honestly don't think that any carp will fail to fall for its charms!

Place your rig in the spoon.

These spoons are ideal for 'slop' or 'groundbait'-type mixes.

Add your chosen
free bait over
the rig.

Slide out into
position.

Twist to drop the free bait and
rig exactly where you want it.

The rig perfectly placed amid a
cloud of attraction. What carp
could resist?

When it all comes right

Catching fish in the margins is a hugely enjoyable process. The runs are usually high in excitement, and you often get to see the carp pick your hookbait and then high-tail it out of the swim to the accompaniment of a shrieking alarm. But landing a fish that's been stalked in the edge is actually far from easy, and a few little wrinkles will help stack the odds very much in your favour. But first, before I let Brian Skoyles show you how to do it, I'm going to briefly mention how *not* to do it.

If you want to stalk carp in the same way that you would legering for them at 100 yards, then I think it's safe to say stalking isn't for you. You can't place baits in the edge and then retire to your chair ten yards away, casually tune in the radio and wait for a run. By the time you've reacted to a bite the fish will have already charged 20 yards, and if there are any weed beds or snags it can find then it'll already have done so. Your chances of landing the carp will taken a severe hit.

As you'll see, you need to sit right next to the rod. You can watch the line for signs of fish, and in some swims you'll actually see the fish pick up the bait, which means you can react to the bite far quicker than even the fish do.

I know that sounds crazy – how can you possibly react faster than a fish that's hooked itself against a leger just six inches away? But trust me, it is possible. More often than not a fish takes a split second to realise what's going on, and by that time you can already be making a grab for the rod. If you get the upper hand in a fight from the word go you can often stop a fish getting up a full head of steam and can keep it on a fairly short line.

This is where the action of rods, like my beloved Fox Twig rods, comes into its own – they're super-strong six-foot long elastic bands, and they absorb every thrust of the carp's power. Yes, the fish can thrash around a lot, but they can't build up a head of steam. You remain in total control, and something radical needs to happen to give the initiative to the carp.

So sit close to the rod, hands poised and muscles at the ready. That way, the minute a fish approaches your bait you're ready for fireworks to start, as Brian Skoyles found out on a recent short stalking session:

1 Gently swing the rig, or cup it, into place. Likely spots are reed beds, lilies or weed beds.

2 The rod is placed on the rod rest with the bale arm open so that the line is slack and has time to settle in the water.

171

3 The rod lock is secured over the rod rest as extra security if there's a screaming take.

4 A few bits of boilies and pellets are also thrown in. It can be a good idea to keep doing this periodically, as it provokes interest from small fish, which in turn attract the carp.

5 The trap is set, with the line drooping into the water. The weight of the rig will do the self-hooking, not the tightness of the line.

6 The bail arm is closed and the clutch checked. Set the clutch according to the swim being fished.

7 Take a vantage point close to the rod and watch for line twitches, a sure sign of fish in the area. Occasionally there will be a spots where you can't see the rig, so be vigilant. Few stalkers take a chair, but it can be a good idea – if you're comfy you won't move and scare the fish.

8 All systems go. The line tightens but I'm already on it, stopping the fish in its tracks. With the rod held low and to the side, the fish can't get a straight pull on the line.

9 The fight is fraught and furious as the carp careers around looking for sanctuary.

10 The carp's inability to build up a head of steam means it's destined for the net.

11 In it goes, caught within 5ft of the bank.

12 Say cheese! All smiles for the camera. The magic of the margins!

You should by now be well on the way to being a very proficient carp angler. At this stage I could try to baffle you with science or invent a load of flannel that makes carp fishing sound an awful lot more difficult than it really is. But I'm not going to do that. I'm a firm believer in keeping your fishing as simple as possible. While there are, of course, advanced skills and bits of kit that are well beyond the scope of a book like this, just be aware that some things attract more anglers than fish!

Anyway, that said, here are ten great ideas that move us on from what we've already discussed, to put more fish in your net:

Glug bag

I rarely go fishing without my glug-pots.

Tecni-spice, my all-time favourite.

Tecni-spice in the glug just soak up the flavour. New ones on the left, years old ones on the right … fish love them!

I always carry a small bag containing a range of special high-attract hook baits soaking in liquid attractors. I purposely pick my hook baits so that they have a range of different smells. As I've mentioned, some of the flavoured baits are literally ten years old, but I just keep the attractor topped up to stop them going mouldy. I don't use them all the time, but when called upon this rescue bag provides baits that can

I'm not the only one with a 'rescue bag' of glugs. Brian is also a big fan of glugs, and he has even more than me … I must try harder!

stack with others and offer a source of attraction that's irresistible.

The Solar's Pot Shot range is outstanding, but my oldest glugged attractor baits are Nutrabaits Tecni-spice ready-made boilies. These boilies have been soaking in Nutrabaits Bait Soak Complex flavoured with Sweet Nutraspice. I've used them for over a decade now and the fish still love them, especially in autumn through to late spring. My all-time favourite cold-water boilie.

So get yourself a small glug bag. It doesn't take up a lot of space, but it's a little bag that can make a big difference.

Your glug bag doesn't have to be big and bulky to make an impressive difference.

Get ziggy

Zigs are all the rage these days, and not without very good reason. They've been responsible for the capture of an awful lot of carp.

You can trim a pop-up, use a bit of foam or a plastic imitation bait. I usually use the trimmed pop-up or the bit of foam.

In a nutshell a zig rig is simply a buoyant hookbait presented on a very long hooklink that pops into mid-water, say five 5ft deep in a 7ft deep swim. It's worth experimenting with what depth you fish a zig, but a good starting point is two-thirds of the actual depth. Using a fine nylon hooklink and a cut-down pop-up boilie positioned directly on the back of the hook is generally the best way to a catch a mid-water swimmer.

This isn't a summer-only method when you're fishing for cruising fish, as some people suggest. Many carp can be caught in mid-water in winter, when they're drifting around in the most stable conditions where freezing temperatures make little difference.

All sorts of hookbaits can work. It's worth trying a cut-down boilie, a piece of shaped foam or one of the new Nash's Zig Bugs. They all work.

Casting can be an issue with long zigs. I tend to place the hookbait in a bucket or on an unhooking mat, to make sure nothing catches on the cast.

It can also be a problem playing fish on a long zig with a heavy lead, so where possible I use a small lead and encourage it to drop-off on the take, by not using a tail rubber to hold it in place. Instead I just tie a small length of PVA string around the lead clip to hold the lead in place on the cast.

Fox Zig Aligna kit

On the subject of zig rigging, have a look at this superb idea from Fox. It presents a piece of high-density foam tight to the back of the hook in the perfect position to snare a fish sucking in the bait. Simply:

1 Take your length of hooklink line and tie on your hook.

2 Slide on an Aligna.

3 Push it into position over the hook eye and knot.

4 Cut off a short length of foam.

5 Push it into the small plastic holder and locate the holder in the Aligna.

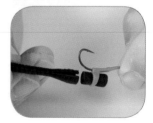

6 Push the plastic holder through the Aligna and it leaves the foam in position.

It's a classic case of a brilliant bit of thinking delivering a simple solution to a fish-catching problem.

Balanced hookbaits

Balancing hookbaits is a great tactic to fool the more experienced fish.

Tweaking the rig and hookbait to take away the weight of the hook and line, and make the hook behave just like the freebies, is a simple but very important idea.

There are many ways of doing it.

You can tip a sinking boilie with a buoyant one to negate the weight of the sinking bait.

It's also a good idea to drill a boilie out and plug the bait with a piece of cork to achieve the same effect, and by varying the size of the cork plug you can adjust the buoyancy.

You can also make some of the larger particles, such as Tiger Nuts, have neutral buoyancy by drilling and cork plugging.

Just remember to test your hookbait before casting out, to make sure you've achieved the level of buoyancy you want. With a bit of care you can get baits to virtually 'hover' in the water; consequently they're often called 'wafters', as the fish waft them as they move past them.

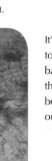

It's important to check your bait sits right in the water before casting out.

Bait boats

Controversial, this one, and if I had my way every single bait boat would be torpedoed! But my loathing of them doesn't alter the fact that they can be very effective fish catchers, either when placing baits beyond your casting range or for pinpoint bait placement with the minimum of disturbance. Bait boats do help catch more carp … but I still hate them!

Love 'em or hate 'em, it can't be denied that used properly and sensibly bait boats can give you a huge edge.

One big advantage of bait boats is that you can get very sloppy mixes exactly where you want them with the minimum of disturbance.

A lovely cloud of attraction for fish to home-in on.

Supermarket baits

Sweetcorn is one of the best carp baits around … full stop!

Mussels have accounted for large numbers of carp over the years.

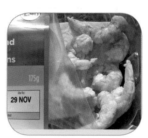

On the quiet, prawns have caught some very big carp. You might get a bonus big perch as well, but don't mention big perch to me!

In the colder months Peperami comes into it's own.

Your local supermarket can provide a wide range of very, very good alternative carp baits.

Most carpers get their baits from their local tackle shop or their favourite bait supplier, but your local supermarket may well have a whole range of baits just sitting on the shelf waiting for you. These days it's not so fashionable to use basic supermarket baits, but since when have carp been aware of angling trends? You can find everything from the obvious tins of sweetcorn and luncheon meat, to cockles, mussels, prawns, Peperami, sausage meat, meatballs, dog foods, cat foods, bread, marshmallows, nuts and seeds.

And don't think of these as second-class baits – they make brilliant alternative baits if you want to be a little bit different. I know of several very successful carpers who use nothing else … they just keep very quiet about it!

Pop-Up Pegs

This idea from Ace is a cracker, and is ideal for presenting chod rigs or pop-up rigs of any sort. The bait simply twists on to the screw and the rest is history. It's easy, it works, and it makes it easier to bait up a variety of rigs.

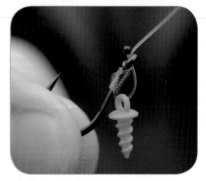

A brilliant idea from Ace, so simple but so effective.

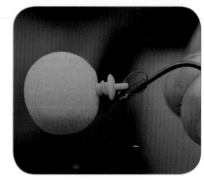

Easy to use – just screw your bait on.

Foam it up

Solar Tackle make a product that will no doubt draw laughs, but for my fishing it's invaluable. What is it? It's foam. Yep, I know, how can that be a product for carp fishing? Let me explain.

I wrap foam around my hookbait before casting out so that it won't plunge deep into the rubbish cluttering the lake bed and snare the hookbait. When the foam dissolves it releases the hookbait, which slowly settles to the bottom, while the leftover foam rises to the surface, marking the spot

for your loose feed. A genuine double-bonus!

I 'foam-up' even if I'm using PVA mesh bags or stringers. It gives me confidence that my hook hasn't caught any weed on the way down.

Ian Russell has told me about a heavily weeded lake that he emptied when he attached a PVA bag containing two pop-ups to his rig before casting out. When the bag melted the two pop-ups rose to the surface, allowing the hookbait to slowly drift to the bottom.

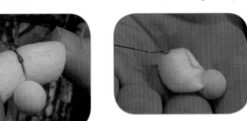

Lay the foam behind the hook.

Slightly dampen one side with your tongue, then fold over and press gently.

Ian Russell told me about some stunning fish that he caught using the foaming-up technique.

Raking a swim

Swims that are choked with weed can be very productive but are often ignored because of the underwater forest. But if you tie a really heavy rake head to a strong rope and throw it in the lake, the rake head sinks, bites into the weed, and

you can then pull it out, ripping the weed with it.

Not only does this colour up the water, it also tears out some of the weed and frees up food that was clinging to the vegetation. It's an overlooked method but a very good one.

Raking a swim can be hard work but is well worth it.

A lot of anglers are put off fishing 'underwater jungles'.

The rake clears normally unfishable areas and frees-up food, and fish just have to investigate.

Going natural

Don't ignore maggots and worms. Over the years they've caught thousands of carp.

Small PVA bags of maggots can be very effective, particularly in winter.

Worms and maggots are a great bait for bream and roach but useless for carp, right? Well actually, no – especially in colder weather in late autumn, winter and early spring.

Tying a small metal ring to the hair below your hook allows you to thread a host of baits on a length of braid and then tie them to the hook. Adding around ten real grubs and a couple of fake buoyant ones is a good plan, as is baiting the hook with a piece of chopped worm then adding the maggots below that. Buying natural baits by the pint might be something match anglers do, but that doesn't mean we can't learn something from them.

PVA-bagging a small bag of maggots can be a great addition to the hookbait. When you get fish feeding hard on maggots it's a great method.

In the summer months a large, juicy lobworm fished under a float in the margins has caught me plenty of decent carp, and it's truly exciting fishing as that float silently disappears and the water erupts in front of you!

Thread several maggots on to a length of fine braid.

Tie off the ends...

...then tie to rig ring on your hook hair.

A large juicy lobworm has tempted many a large carp!

And finally...

My friends and I have fished intimate margins and mighty rivers. We've been to mysterious canals and stalked overgrown treelines, searched local rivers and travelled to far-off foreign lakes. We've sat in anticipation through many a misty dawn, and landed fish for each other as the sun went down.

These are the magical moments and memories that are all part of the emotional rollercoaster that is carp fishing. I've loved every moment of it.

The last tip in this book might seem a bit flippant, but it's honestly meant, and I hope it's taken that way.

While the latest rig ideas, wonderbaits and tackle developments can bring genuine advancement to your fishing, they aren't the solution. What you see, and what you learn along the way, is of much greater importance. Get to know your quarry, and if you can work out what the carp are doing, and when they're likely to do it, you'll be a far better carper and catch far more fish. Gradually you'll develop that vital piece of the carp-catching skill that can't be bought, but only acquired over time ...watercraft.

It might be a long journey, but trust me, it'll be worth it!

Kevin Green

A stunning common. Fish like this are always worth the effort.

My personal best carp – 58lb of pure magic!

IT'S KNOT DIFFICULT

The chance to catch the carp of your dreams won't come along every trip, but when that day does arrive, and that very special fish makes a mistake and picks up your hookbait, you want to be sure that it ends up in the landing net. You can have the best rods and reels in the world, but if your knots let you down then your special memory could be lost forever.

Selecting the right knot and, just as importantly, tying it correctly are both *vital*. An angry carp making a last-ditch break for freedom will test your gear to the limit. It's quite likely that you'll have up to three knots in your tackle set-up, so it's important you get all of them right.

Hopefully this knot guide will help. The list isn't definitive by any means, but if you master tying the eight knots I've listed you'll be in a position to effectively tackle up in the vast majority of situations in which you'll find yourself.

First of all, a few general rules to reliable knot tying:

Check the line thoroughly first

It's often the last metre or so of line that takes the most stick in general use, so before tying the rig/leader on just do a quick check. Wet your fingers and slowly slide them down the line. If there are any slight nicks, signs of wear etc, cut it off.

■ Make sure any loops or coils bed down evenly

As you're tying your knots, make sure all the loops and coils are even. That way the pressure through the knot is also even. Uneven coils can squash each other and lead to failure of the knot overall.

■ Always moisten a knot as you tighten it

Most knots will tighten smoothly, but moistening them first will reduce the friction in the knot and make it even easier. Take your time, and tease the knot together rather than rushing it.

■ If it doesn't look right, cut it off and do it again

No matter how experienced you are, from time to time a knot will go wrong. Under close examination it just doesn't look right. Don't take any chances – it doesn't take long to cut it off and redo it.

■ Tag-end length

Several knots rely on the end of the line being tucked back through a loop (the blood knot, for example), so don't cut the tag end too close to the loop – it isn't necessary, and the closer you cut it the greater the chance that under pressure it will come out and the knot will unravel.

■ Test it with a steady pull

It's a good idea to test a knot once you've tied it. Apply steady pressure, rather than a snatch. Several companies make hook pullers that enable you to test hook knots as well, without the risk of getting the hook in your finger!

■ Protection

To give your knot the best chance of surviving the pressures it will be under, it's a good idea to protect it in some way. Shrink-tube and fine-diameter silicone tubing are both excellent for this.

The overhand loop knot

The simplest of knots and ideal for tying the tiny loop needed on the end of the hair. I wouldn't recommend this knot for anything else, and certainly not for any part of a rig that'll be taking the full stress of playing a fish. A nice little tip if you're struggling to make the loop very small, is, before you pull it tight, to put a needle in the knot itself and use it to slide the knot closer to the end, then transfer the needle into the actual end loop and pull tight.

1 Fold a short length of line back on to itself.

2 Fold both to make a small circle and pass the end around both pieces of line and through the hole.

3 Tease small and then pull tight.

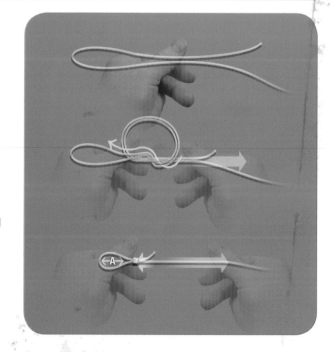

The knotless knot or 'no-knot'

… so called because on closer inspection there really isn't any knot to speak of. Very simple to tie, very easy to get the hair length spot on, so very popular. A very reliable knot that's easy to tie.

1 Tie a small loop in the end of your chosen hooklength line.

2 Thread the line through the back of the hook eye and adjust the hair length to suit the bait you intend to use.

3 Whip down the shank (normally six to eight turns).

4 Holding the turns tight, bring the line back and again thread it through the back of the hook.

5 Pull tight.

A couple of things worth mentioning. When starting the knotless knot it's important that you thread the line from the outside of the hook, and that after whipping down the shank you also come back through the hook eye from the outside to complete the knot, as this makes the hook turn correctly in the fish's mouth. The knotless knot is excellent on the more supple hooklengths such as braid or stripped-back coated braid but can be less effective on stiffer lines, as it stops the hook and bait moving freely in the fish's mouth.

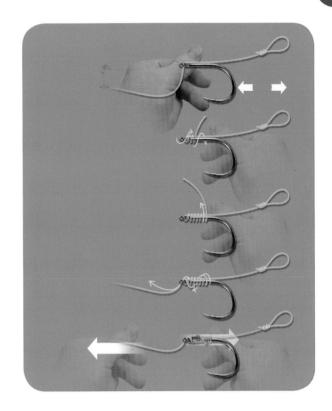

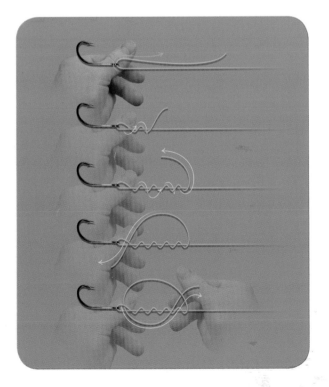

The tucked blood knot

The tucked blood or swivel knot is a very popular knot, but you need to take care that you do tuck it, as without the tuck it's prone to slip under pressure. It's also advisable not to trim the tag end too short, as the whole knot relies on this tag end not coming un-tucked. It can be used to tie on hooks, swivels and links etc, but isn't personally my 'first-choice' knot for this (see grinner knot).

1 Thread the line through the eye of the swivel or hook etc.

2 Make turns back around the line (six to eight is average).

3 Bring the end of the line back and thread it through the first gap…

4 …then tuck the end through the loop you've just formed.

5 Moisten and ease tight, then trim off any excess line.

The grinner knot

One of my favourite knots, which I use in preference to the tucked blood. Slightly harder to learn, but well worth the effort in terms of reliability and overall knot strength.

1 Thread the line through the eye of the swivel or hook etc.

2 Form a loop and start to make turns with the end, through the loop and around the centre line.

3 Repeat this for approximately six to eight turns.

4 Moisten and ease the loop together.

5 Slide the knot down to the swivel or hook, pull tight and trim off tag end.

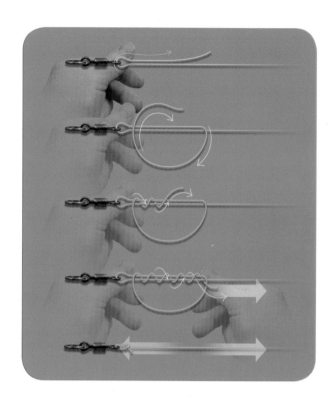

The Palomar knot

Possibly my favourite knot of all, easy to tie and very reliable, plus it doesn't leave any slight kinks in the line as it comes away from the hook or swivel etc. I also like the fact that it automatically gives you two loops through the hook eye or swivel, which again I think improves reliability.

1 Tuck the line through the swivel eye or hook eye then bring it back through.

2 Produce a single overhand loop knot with the hook or swivel in the knot itself.

3 Take the end of the loop and push it over the hook or swivel.

4 Moisten and tease the knot together. You might have to pull the line and/or the tag end separately to get the knot to form properly.

5 Pull tight and trim off the tag end.

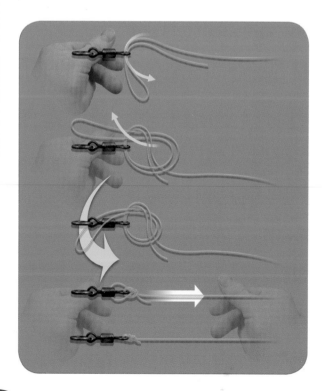

The leader knot

There are several leader knots to pick from, and they all have their devotees. This is my favourite. It's reliable, and great for tying together two lines of different diameters – ideal on your marker and spod rod/reel set-ups.

1 Form a simple open loop in the thicker leader line.

2 Pass the tag end twice through the loop.

3 Pull it almost closed so it forms a figure of eight.

4 Pass your thinner reel line through the first hole and out through the second.

5 Pull the figure of eight closed.

6 Using the thinner line, do a grinner knot around the thicker line.

7 Tease it tight.

8 Moisten and pull the two knots together, then trim off the two tag ends.

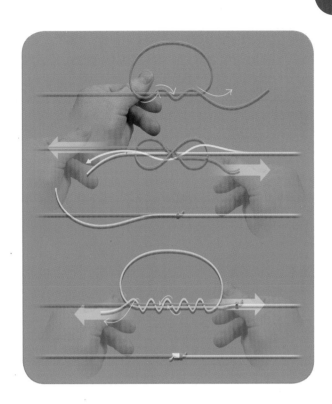

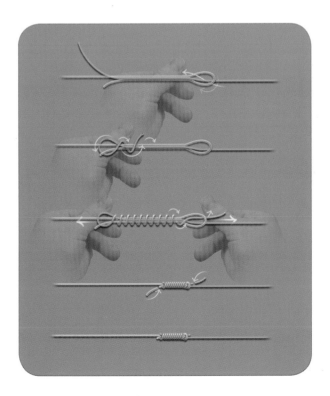

The Albright knot

Not the easiest knot in the world to master but another one where it's well worth making the effort. It's perfect for combi rigs. I usually add a drop of rig glue to this knot as an added precaution to stop any chance of it slipping.

1 Double back the thicker line to form a flat loop, then thread the second line through it.

2 Create turns back toward the end of the loop.

3 Do this for eight to ten turns depending on the thickness of the line, then tuck the spare through the loop.

4 Moisten and tease together.

5 Pull tight, and trim off tag ends.

The Snell or whipping knot

This knot is tricky to tie but necessary for the reverse hair and variations of the chod rig and stiff rig. Once again it's well worth making the effort.

1 Take approximately 30cm of fine hair braid and trap a bait band in a small overhand loop at one end, then lay it along the hook shank and form a large loop.

2 Make turns back along the hook shank, trapping the tag end as you do so.

3 Hold the turns and pull the tag end so the larger loop disappears.

4 Push up to the eye and trim off the tag end.

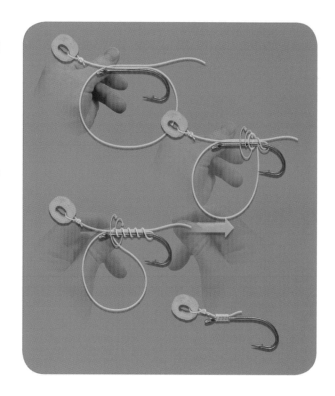

The slip knot or stop knot

Ideal for marking your line so that you can clip up and recast to the same spot easily, and consequently also known as a marker knot. I prefer to use short lengths of pole elastic for this, as it doesn't damage the line and is clearly visible on the spool.

1 Form a loop along the mainline.

2 Take one end and make four or five turns through the loop and around the line.

3 Pull both ends to close the loop. Keep the mainline straight as you do this.

4 Tighten the knot and trim off the tag ends. Don't trim them off too short, as you want to be able to see the knot clearly.

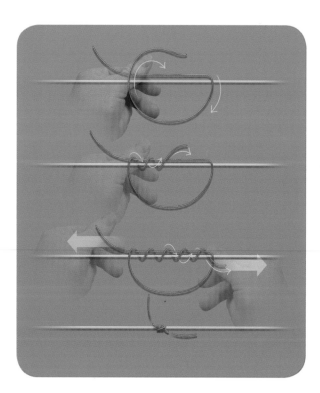

GLOSSARY

Action – The bending of a rod when casting or playing a fish.

Attractor bait – Bait designed to carry flavours that attract carp.

Backing – Technique in which you wind on some old line and tape over it, so that you use less actual reel line each time you spool up.

Bail arm – The wire element of a fixed-spool reel that guides the line.

Bait boat – A remote-controlled boat used to place free offerings or a baited rig at a distance that can't be achieved by more conventional means.

Bait floss – Fine thread used to tie the hookbait to the rig ring.

Bait rocket – Bait-loaded plastic tube with a buoyant nosecone that causes it to turn upside down when it hits the water. Also known as a 'spod'.

Baitrunner – A reel with a second clutch system that disengages the spool clutch. Originally introduced by Shimano, who marketed such reels under the 'Baitrunner' name.

Bank stick – Adjustable metal pole with a spike at the bottom for pushing into the ground, and a thread at the top to which a rod rest can be screwed.

Big pit reels – Nickname for 10,000-size reels.

Bite alarm – Electronic device that replaces the front rod rest and signals line movement.

Bivvy – The small tent used by fishermen, usually when fishing overnight.

Boilie – Bait consisting of small balls of boiled dough usually made with eggs, milk protein powder and/or fishmeal and bird food. Flavours and colour can also be added.

Boilie needle – A needle device with a hook or barb on the end that's pushed through the bait, enabling the loop on the hair to be pulled back through the bait.

Boilie stop – Small plastic stop that slots into the hair loop to stop the bait sliding off.

Braid blades – Strong, thin-bladed, very sharp scissors used to cut braided line.

Buzzer – Alternative name for an electronic bait alarm.

Clutch – Tensioning device fitted in a reel to control how line is released when pulled from a reel by a hooked fish. Also called the 'drag'.

Combi or **combo** – A combination, of lines as in a combi rig, or of bait as in, for example, a boilie/corn combo.

Controller – A large, buoyant float that provides cast weight when surface fishing.

Crashing – The leaping and rolling of carp near the surface. Also called 'topping'.

Drag – Tensioning device fitted in a reel. Also called the 'clutch'.

Drop-back bite – A bite in which the fish picks up the bait and swims back towards the angler, causing the line to go slack.

Flying backlead – A small leger weight running on the mainline between the rig and the rod. Designed to sink the line to keep it out of sight.

Free offerings or **freebies** – Food scattered as a lure in the area being fished. Also referred to as 'loosefeed'.

Glugs – Nickname for flavoured solutions poured on boilies.

Groundbait – Bait thrown into the water to attract fish to an area.

Growlers – An alternative name for tiger nuts.

Guides – The rings on a rod through which the line runs. Also known as 'rod rings'.

Hair rig – Set-up in which the bait isn't attached directly to the hook but instead hangs from a short length of fine line just below it. Gets its name from originally being made from human hair.

Hanger – An indicator that hangs on the line to reveal line movement.

HNV – High nutritional value. Descriptive term applied to boilies with a range of ingredients designed to provide all the carp's dietary needs.

Hooklink or **hooklength** – The short length of line at the bottom of a rig carrying the hook. Also known as a 'hook-to-nylon', 'trace' or 'tail'. It's usually slightly weaker than the mainline.

Lead – Common name for a leger.

Lead clip rig – Leger rig from which the weight can be jettisoned in an emergency.

Leadcore – A lead wire core covered in a woven braid sheath. Designed to pin the line to the bottom, it has the added benefit of reducing the risk of tangles.

Leader – A length of often stronger line that's placed between the mainline and the rig system. Its use is mainly twofold – to provide increased resistance to abrasion and to improve presentation. See also 'shock leader'.

Leading around – Nickname given to the technique of casting a lead or lead/marker float out and dragging it back to gain clues as to the make-up of the lake bottom.

Leger – A weight attached to the mainline to give it adequate casting weight; commonly called a 'lead'.

Line bites – Twitches and pulls on the line caused by large fish bumping into it.

Mag aligner rig – Rig that uses a rubber maggot to mask the hook, add buoyancy and create an angle near the hook eye.

Mainline – An alternative name for reel line.

Marker float – A large, buoyant float that's cast out and then rises to the surface, indicating position, depth etc.

Pads – Lily pads. Usually excellent fish-holding areas.

Particle – Generic name given to a range of baits that tend to be small. In certain conditions they can be introduced in larger quantities to generate preoccupied feeding.

187

Peg – The part of the water that you've decided to fish. Also called a 'swim'.

Plumbing – Measuring the depth of the water.

Pop-up – A boilie bait specifically designed to pop up from or float above the lake bed.

PVA – Poly vinyl acetate.

Rig – The assembled tackle attached to the end of the line that's cast into the water.

Rig rings – Small stainless steel rings used to present bait tight to the back of a hook.

Rod pod – A stand-alone frame that can hold two or three rods complete with bite alarms and rod rests.

Rod rings – The rings on a rod through which the line runs. Also known as 'guides'.

Shelf-life boilies – Boilies that have been treated with a preservative or undergone a special process during manufacture to stop them going mouldy.

Shock leader – When casting larger leads with considerable force it's essential to use a 'shock leader' at least ten times the weight of the lead being utilised, and long enough to put several turns of line on the reel. Basically a shock absorber.

Sleeve – Small length of thin tubing at the top of the hooklink to prevent tangles.

Snag – Any obstruction in the water that traps a fishing line.

Specimen fish – An imprecise term for a big fish, that varies across species and venues. For example, on some lakes a 20-pounder may be small, but on most venues it would rank as a specimen!

Spod – Bait-loaded plastic tube with a buoyant nosecone that causes it to turn upside down when it hits the water. Also known as a 'bait rocket'.

Spodding – Using a spod or spomb to introduce feed further out into a swim than can be reached by means of a catapult.

Spomb – Recent type of spod shaped like a bomb. Its halves are designed to spring apart on impact with the water.

Stiff rig – A rig that utilises a nylon hooklength.

Strike – Angler's reaction to a bite on the line – the 'swish' of the rod to make the connection between fish and hook.

Swim – The part of the water that you've decided to fish. Also called a 'peg'.

Tag end – The short length of line left when spare line is cut off during knot tying.

Tail – The short length of line at the bottom of a float rig carrying the hook. Also known as a 'hooklink', 'hooklength', 'hook-to-nylon' or 'trace'.

Test curve rating or **TC** – Measurement of the weight that's needed to bend the tip of a rod through 90°.

Topping – The leaping and rolling of carp near the surface. Also called 'crashing'.

Wafter – A hookbait of neutral buoyancy that fish waft as they move past it.

Zig rig – A super-long hooklink baited with a very buoyant pop-up boilie that floats in the mid to upper layers of the water column.

Credits

Author
Kevin Green

Project Manager
Louise McIntyre

Copy Editor
Ian Heath

Page Design
James Robertson

Photography
Mick Rouse
With additional pictures from
Lloyd Rogers
Steve Broad
Graham Drewery
Brian Skoyles
Bill Cottam

Illustrations
Dave Batten (Hooklinks)

The author would also like to thank the following companies for their support in the production of this book.

Avid Carp
Daiwa Sports
ESP Carpgear
Fox International
Hinders Fishing Superstore
Korda (Thinking Tackle)
Nash Tackle
Nutrabaits
Rollin Baits Ltd.
Solar Tackle

Haynes Publishing would like to thank Brian Skoyles and Mick Rouse for helping to complete Kevin's book. We know they did it for Kevin, but we couldn't have published it without them. Our thoughts are with Kevin's family and we hope that one day his sons will enjoy reading and learning from his books.